Coinage and society in Britain and Gaul: some current problems

edited by Barry Cunliffe

1981

Research Report No 38

The Council for British Archaeology

Copyright © 1981 The Council for British Archaeology

Published by the Council for British Archaeology
112 Kennington Road
London SE11 6RE
Printed by Henry Ling Ltd, The Dorset Press, Dorchester

British Library Cataloguing in Publishing Data

Coinage and society in Britain and Gaul.
  – (Research report/Council for British Archaeology,
  ISSN 0589-9036; no. 38)
  1. Coinage – Great Britain – History – Congresses
  2. Coinage – France – History – Congresses
  I. Cunliffe, Barry   II. Council for British
  Archaeology
  332.4'9'0941   HG933

ISBN 0-906780-04-7

Contents

Contents

The Oxford Department of External Studies has, in recent years, held three Iron Age conferences each designed to examine the most recent British work against its Continental background. The first, which took place in October 1975, was concerned with oppida and the beginnings of urbanization in barbarian Europe; the second, in October 1977, dealt with Lowland Iron Age communities in Europe, while the third, held in October 1978, covered the theme of early coinage and society in Britain and Gaul. It is a selection of the papers presented at this last, suitably augmented, which forms the basis of the present volume.

It was clear, as a result of the 1975 conference, that in the field of early coinage the new work of Simone Scheers and John Kent was having a significant effect on our understanding of the Late pre-Roman Iron Age in Britain. It was also evident that some diversity of opinion in the problems of interpretation was beginning to develop. This was exemplified by the contrast in the approach of John Collis and of Warwick Rodwell, who had just completed a detailed study of the Trinovantes and Catuvellauni. Since much needed to be discussed at length, it was decided to devote the 1978 conference wholly to problems of early coinage.

Keith Rutter and Richard Reece were invited to discuss the Greek and Roman background respectively; Simone Scheers and Daphne Nash considered recent work in France; John Kent and the writer examined aspects of the British scene; while John Collis, Colin Haselgrove, and Mansel Spratling dealt with more theoretical matters. The present papers are based substantially upon these contributions but with modifications and additions.

The additions may be briefly justified. Much time was spent at the conference in discussing the quality of the coin data. To display some of the hidden snares and delusions in our distribution maps Warwick Rodwell has kindly provided a sample study of the Essex coin finds—a salutary reminder to those who wish to expose such data to sophisticated spatial analysis of the severe limitations of which they ought to be aware. We have also added some up-to-date distribution maps, based on evidence available up to October 1978, in the hope that they will be of some general use.

One point remains to be emphasized. The study of Celtic coins in Britain depends entirely on the maintenance of an adequate record of all finds. I have therefore taken this opportunity of inviting my colleague Professor Sheppard Frere to contribute a note on the National Index of Celtic Coins maintained at the Institute of Archaeology at Oxford. Professor Frere writes:

'The Coin Index contains a card for each coin recorded, on which details of find-spot, ownership, weight, and type are inscribed, and a photograph affixed of each face of the coin, preferably at a scale of 2 : 1. The photographs are particularly important since pre-Roman coins are struck in a by no means standard way; each coin has individual characteristics, whether of eccentricity of the die on the flan or of flaws round the edge, which serve to distinguish it from others in the same series. Thus the identity of individual coins can be established and maintained from their photographs in addition, of course, to the possibility of die studies.

'The Coin Index contains at present about 10 000 cards. Its value greatly increases as it becomes more comprehensive, but since the death of D F Allen, to whom the majority of new discoveries were normally submitted, the compilers have had to rely much more upon the goodwill of correspondents for information on new discoveries. Good relations exist with the Ashmolean and Devizes Museums amongst others, and information is passed on, but in recent years little information has been received of discoveries reported at the British Museum, to which, of course, the largest number naturally come. It is hoped that this flaw in the arrangements will soon be set right. Arrangements exist for coins which are sent for identification either to the Institute of Archaeology at Oxford or to the Ashmolean Museum to be photographed and prints sent free of charge to the owner or excavator. Where coins cannot be so submitted, the compilers will gladly pay for prints or arrange for a visit by the Institute's photographer.'

Contributors

J R Collis, MA, PhD, Department of Ancient History, University of Sheffield.

Professor B W Cunliffe, MA, PhD, LittD, FBA, FSA, Institute of Archaeology, Oxford.

C Haselgrove, BA, Department of Archaeology, University of Durham.

J P C Kent, BA, PhD, FSA, Department of Coins and Medals, British Museum, London.

Ms D Nash, BA, DPhil, Ashmolean Museum, Oxford.

R M Reece, BSc, DPhil, FSA, Institute of Archaeology, London.

W J Rodwell, PhD, FSA, Director of the Committee for Rescue Archaeology in Avon, Gloucestershire and Somerset (CRAAGS), Mark Lane, Bristol.

N K Rutter, MA, PhD, Department of Greek, University of Edinburgh.

Ms S Scheers, PhD, University of Leuven, Belgium.

Early Greek coinage and the influence of the Athenian state

Keith Rutter

In a recently published paper, the late Derek Allen posed some fundamental questions about the nature and functions of coinages in Celtic Europe (Allen 1976). Starting from the proposition that an imitative coinage will never have been more sophisticated than the coinage which it imitated, Allen applied to the Celtic world some of the methods and results of research into the nature of coinages on the Mediterranean coast, to challenge the assumption that Celtic coins existed to serve the interests of Celtic trade. The narrow distributions of Celtic coins, at least the early ones, and the nature of ancient trade itself combine to suggest that 'The primary function of Celtic coinage in precious metals must be sought within the communities to which they were confined', and that '. . . the main purpose underlying the coinage of money was to facilitate compliance with the requirements of the complicated social structure of Celtic life' (Allen 1976, 200–1). But Allen did not deny that a medium of exchange introduced for one purpose may not subsequently have been found useful and convenient in other contexts. To judge from the conclusions set out in Allen's short paper, the application to one field of ancient coinage of results achieved in another is potentially very fruitful, and it may be that what I have to say about Athenian coinage will help to illuminate some of the problems of the Celtic coinages. This is not, however, to suggest that comparisons should be all one way. The nature and functions of Greek coinages are themselves the subjects of much speculation, in which comparisons with the practices of other times and places are a fruitful source of ideas. I think, for example, of Professor Grierson's discussion of commerce in the 'Dark Ages', with his suggestion that in the distribution of wealth—goods or coin—the alternatives to trade were more important than trade itself; though, with so many alternatives available, the difficulty lies in estimating their importance (Grierson 1959; 1961; 1977).

The first 150 years or so of Athenian coinage, that is, from about the middle of the 6th century BC to the end of the 5th, provide plenty of opportunities to discuss in some depth problems of wider interest: I shall be able to draw particular attention to problems connected with the metals used for coins, the sources of those metals, the range of denominations, circulation, and function and use. But there is little point in discussing such problems without an accurate chronological framework, and here there is at once a difficulty, for it is still not possible to provide a continuous history of the first 150 years of Athenian coinage whose details would command universal assent. However, I believe that although areas of dispute remain, such progress has been made recently in elucidating the chronology of early Athenian coinage that it is not premature to attempt the synthesis of the results with the literary and epigraphic record, uniquely ample in the Greek world, relating to institutions, use, and attitudes.

But before I embark on a discussion of the nature and chronology of the coinage, I want to introduce, briefly, the other element in my title—the state. At the time when coinage was introduced at Athens—there is unanimity at least that it happened in the 6th century—the Athenian state consisted essentially of the elements ascribed by Thucydides to the legendary king Theseus: it was created by the establishment in Athens itself of a central authority over the previously independent towns of Attica, such as Eleusis; these towns continued to exist as settlements, but

without the institutions of autonomy (Thucydides 2.15.1–2). The cults of Athens, too, came to dominate the religious life of Attica, but it is worth pointing out at this stage that there were sanctuaries outside Athens, as well as inside, whose financial role was not inconsiderable. The sanctuaries of Demeter at Eleusis, Nemesis at Rhamnous, Artemis at Brauron, and Poseidon at Sounion were all the scene of building projects in the 5th century. From Rhamnous, we possess accounts of the money-lending activities of the temple, *c* 450–40 (Meiggs & Lewis 1969, no 53); the mystery cult at Eleusis attracted visitors from far and wide, and in the 4th century and later provided occasions for the actual minting of coins (Thompson 1942). Throughout the period we are considering, the majority of the citizens of Athens were small farmers, working the little fertile ground themselves, frequently with the help of slaves or seasonal labour. Even in 431 most Athenians lived in the country (Thucydides 2.14.2); however, economic, social, and political developments were introducing more diversification in the social structure, more ways of making a living apart from the land. Relations between town and country were close. Countrymen and townsmen were all Athenian citizens, sharing common political institutions. Life for most was hard, tastes frugal. There were, however, some relatively wealthy landowners, and by the beginning of the 6th century tension between them and the poorer farmers had become acute. Solon was appointed to deal with the agrarian crisis in 594/3, but his reforms did not include a redistribution of land, and later in the century there occurred what he had striven to avoid—a period of tyranny, personal rule by an individual. But the reign of Peisistratus especially was looked back on by many as a golden age, and in general the tyranny gave Athens a period of stability in which agriculture and manufacture were fostered, a programme of useful and prestigious public works was initiated, and state festivals were celebrated on a more lavish scale (Aristotle, *AP*, 16.7; Thucydides 6.54.5–6).

Turning now to the coins, there are three categories of early Athenian coinage, forming a progressive sequence of issues.[1] The first contains coins known by convention as *Wappenmünzen* because the types of many of them have sometimes been interpreted as family or personal badges. This interpretation was developed by Seltman (1924, 20–2), but its chief support, the association of triskeles with the Alcmeonidae, has been removed (see Hopper 1960, 242ff). A high proportion of the coins of which we have a record are didrachms, but there are a few tetradrachms and a considerable range of smaller denominations: drachms and obols, and a few trihemiobols, half, and quarter obols. All these coins are of silver, but a few electrum coins are known which may belong to the same series.[2] With some significant exceptions to be discussed shortly, the reverses are struck with a simple punch; the obverses, on the other hand, bear a variety of types: amphora, beetle, bull's head, Gorgoneion, horse, forepart of horse, hindquarter of horse, knucklebone, owl, triskeles, wheel (strutted and unstrutted). A number of arguments combine to prove, first, that the varied types of the *Wappenmünzen* belong to a single series[3] and, secondly, that their place of origin is Athens, rather than Euboea or any other possible mint in central Greece.[4] There is not enough evidence to put the *Wappenmünzen* into any convincing relative order, except at the end, when there is a significant development on the reverses of didrachm dies coupled with obverse Gorgoneion: the upper quarter of the incuse square is filled with a small facing lion's head, the first hint of a full reverse type. Such a lion type appears pretty soon on the reverses of the first tetradrachms, again with obverse Gorgoneion: note here the way the lion's head is set neatly in a shallow incuse square, surrounded by a wide flattened area of metal. This flattened reverse technique is very similar to that of some coins in the second of our categories: coins with the unvarying types of obverse helmeted head of Athena, reverse owl: note the incuse square surrounded by a wide area of flattened metal.[5] Following Aristophanes, (*Birds* 1106–8), we call these coins 'owls'. Within this category of archaic 'owls' there is considerable variety of fabric, design, and style, providing criteria for subdivision into groups, but always on the obverses the bowl of Athena's helmet lacks any decoration.[6] In the third category, though the types (Athena/owl) remain the same, the *obv* helmet bowl is decorated with upright olive leaves and, at least on tetradrachms, a small crescent is placed behind the owl on the reverse.

Wappenmünzen, 'owls' without leaves, 'owls' with leaves: when were they issued? There is now general agreement that the type of Athena with olive leaves was introduced in the 470s, certainly not before 480.[7] For the thirty years or so after 480, Starr's study provides a detailed guide, until the advent of massive standardized issues in the early 440s. As for the coinage before 480, I take the view, supported by the evidence of hoards, that the 'owl' coinage, with the tetradrachm as the standard coin, was initiated in the last quarter of the 6th century and that it was preceded by the *Wappenmünzen*.[8] The precise date of the change from *Wappenmünzen* to 'owls' is still uncertain. Did it take place before or after the fall of the tyranny in 510? The exploitation of rich deposits of silver in the Athenian mines in the early 5th century certainly allowed the production of a large volume of 'owls' without leaves within a comparatively short space of time (Wallace, W P, 1962, 28–33; Price & Waggoner 1975, 61–4) and the *terminus ante quem* for these coins is 480. As for the date of their introduction, the political confusion immediately following the fall of the tyranny in 510 was hardly a propitious background for a major and lasting innovation in coinage. The suggestion that such an innovation might more appropriately have accompanied the Cleisthenic reforms (508/7)[9] narrows slightly the period allowed for a coinage that was admittedly copious and not necessarily continuous, at least in its earliest stages.[10] The alternative is that the innovation belonged to Hippias, whose family's interest in Athena and her cult is securely attested, at some time in the penultimate decade of the 6th century.[11] What sort of span before that should we allow for the *Wappenmünzen*? It is difficult to imagine for them a period of issue of more than 40, or even 30, years. 125 didrachms survive.[12] There is considerable diversity of obverse types, and between 55 and 62 obverse dies are known; but between 16 and 19 of these are Gorgoneia, coming near the end of the series. The didrachms at least are homogeneous in fabric and minting technique, and were probably introduced around the middle of the 6th century, perhaps by Peisistratus himself after he had finally established his tyranny in 546. The Peisistratids were expelled after 36 years of continuous power.

Athens was among the first of the states of mainland Greece to adopt coinage, along with Aegina and Corinth. The range of denominations is impressive, yet it is unlikely that this coinage was introduced as a general-purpose money, to facilitate market exchanges. The use of the coins in external trade is ruled out because at least in the 6th century their circulation was limited to Attica and Euboea (Thompson *et al* 1973, 2,3,5). Internally, the proper

functioning of subsistence markets for locally produced food, household utensils, and agricultural tools did not require the use of money. However, although Attica in Peisistratus's time was a community in which political status and livelihood depended primarily on the possession of land, this is not to deny that his reign, and that of his sons, saw some increase in the opportunities for making a living in other ways than from the land, in manufacturing, and in the exercise of special skills. Some projects were deliberately fostered by the tyrants—their building programme, for example, or the reconstitution of festivals on a more elaborate scale.[13] Perhaps this is the context for the issue of coins: the number of workers involved in some of these projects encouraged the adoption of a convenient method of payment. The types of the *Wappenmünzen* may give us a clue to the context of their issue. They are not to be regarded as 'clan' or 'family' badges, but many of them show objects or animals that can be associated with the games of the Panathenaic festival: horse, wheel, amphora, owl—even the triskeles as a symbol of speed, the astragalos as a symbol of good or bad luck.[14] Another source of expense for the tyrants were the mercenaries who helped them to introduce and maintain their rule (Parke 1933, 8–9). I shall say a little more later about the possible influence of mercenaries on the issue and circulation of coins, but for the moment I summarize the position in the 6th century by suggesting that coinage was introduced at Athens to serve internal needs, and those official rather than commercial.

At some point in the last twenty years of the 6th century, the character of Athenian coinage changed markedly in several ways. The tetradrachm replaced the didrachm as the standard denomination: indeed, the issue of the latter was discontinued, to be revived only for a brief period in the second quarter of the 5th century. New types were introduced, abandoning the variety of the *Wappenmünzen*, and restricted to *obv* head of Athena, *rev* owl. The origin of the coins was now made explicit by the inclusion of the first three letters of the Athenians' name as part of the *rev* design. The output of the new coins began at a modest level. Variation in details of the types, and in style, may reflect sporadic minting as silver became available, rather than continuous striking from mined metal (Price & Waggoner 1975, 65). Quite soon, however, the picture changes dramatically. Production of coins increased so much that artistic quality declined under the pressure. Recent research, based on a comparative study of hoard evidence, suggests that much of this coinage was issued between 500 and 480, the bulk of it perhaps even more narrowly dated within the decade 490–480. (Price & Waggoner 1975, 56–68).

The background to this development is expenditure by the Athenians on a variety of projects. The years after 510 saw a 'building explosion' at Athens, stimulated in the first instance by the demands of the current constitutional changes, but including, in the early 5th century, temple building, and fortifications at Peiraeus (Boersma 1970, 28–41). The resources to pay for some of this work, particularly in the late 6th century, may have derived from ransom money of two minas per head, received in about 506 for 700 Boeotian prisoners and an unknown number of Chalcidians.[15] Defence against external enemies, in particular the Aeginetans, required expenditure on the building and maintenance of ships, culminating in the decision taken in 483/2 to use a profit of 100 talents of silver accruing from the working of the mines of Laurium to build perhaps 100 triremes (Labarbe 1957; Buchanan 1962, 4–8). Financial policy-making in archaic Athens, as indeed in the rest of the contemporary Greek world, was of a rudimentary nature, and one way of dealing with such a surplus was one that was actually proposed—a distribution among the citizens, at 10 drachmae a head (Herodotus 7.144.1). Themistocles's alternative proposal was to spend the money on ships to combat the Aeginetans. It was not unique in the Greek world. At about the same time or very slightly earlier the Thasians, too, decided to spend revenues from their mines on building ships and strengthening their fortifications (Herodotus 6.46.2–3). These decisions and the measures required to carry them out represent an important step in the development of public finance in the respective cities. When the Persian Mardonius advanced on them in 492, the Thasians submitted without a blow (Herodotus 6.48.1). Athens was more fortunate: her natural endowment, combined with a readiness to exploit it constructively, launched her on her career as a successful naval power.[16] As for the coins, they are a tangible record of the exploitation of Athens's windfall, but it is difficult to assess the precise role they played in it. Themistocles's proposal to spend 100 talents on building ships was carried: some silver was obviously very rapidly coined for this purpose, to pay for skills, or for materials such as timber, metals, pitch, and ruddle. We hear, too, of a cash allowance of 8 drachmae per man distributed to those manning the fleet on the eve of Salamis (Wallace, M B, 1974, 27, n 16). But the hoard evidence indicates that the output of coins started to increase substantially well before 480, and indeed before 483/2, which must be the date of Themistocles's proposal and not of the original discovery of the richer levels of silver (Price & Waggoner 1975, 61–4; Wallace 1962, 28–33). Unfortunately, we know nothing of the precise mechanisms by which the citizen body profited from the mines at this time: whether it leased them, and if it did, how the concession holders paid for their leases; what proportion of the mined silver reached the state treasury, and by what method; at what point the silver acquired was coined.

There can be little doubt, then, that the Athenian coinage of the 30 years or so before 480, particularly ample after 500, was issued to facilitate payments for materials and services in connection with a variety of expensive domestic projects. Much of the raw material required must have been imported from abroad, notably timber from the coasts of Thrace and Macedonia, though such traffic is not reflected in finds of Athenian coins in those areas.[17] However, 'owls' do begin to apear in overseas hoards deposited in the early years of the 5th century, not too long after their introduction, in the western Mediterranean (Italy and Sicily) and in the east (Egypt and the Levant).[18] Early 'owls' turn up also in hoards on 'the trade route from Greece to the East running along the south coast of Asia Minor'.[19] It has been suggested, therefore, that the changes introduced with the 'owl' coinage—the larger standard coin, unvarying types, specific reference to the mint of origin—indicate a coinage 'designed for foreign trade' (Kraay 1976, 60). This implies either that the coins are the residue of individual trading ventures in which they were employed as a medium of exchange (Austin 1970, 38) or—a rather different explanation but still in the commercial field—that Athens exported silver in the form of coins 'strictly for their metallic value as silver, and not as money proper' (Austin & Vidal-Naquet 1977, 57; Finley 1973, 134). The first question is, was the 'owl' coinage *designed* for either or both of these commercial roles?

Whether they were introduced before or after 510, the new types of the 'owl' coinage can be satisfactorily explained in terms of internal Athenian politics.[20] What then of the ethnic? It declares unequivocally the origin of the coins, and its presence might have reassured even the least experienced of foreign merchants, but that sort of consideration was probably not in the minds of the Athenians when they decided to introduce it as part of the

reverse type. They included it not so much to help identification of the coin in international circulation as to authenticate it, like any other public document, to guarantee its official status.[21] The fairly rapid dispersal of new 'owls' coins to certain areas abroad does not mean that their new features—in particular the types and ethnic[22]—were deliberately designed from the start to encourage such dispersal. Furthermore, the earliest 'owls', though of high quality artistically, were not issued in the numbers or with the consistency to suggest that they were capable of fulfilling more than domestic needs (see above). Yet the fact is that the new 'owls' were dispersed—and quite soon after their introduction. Does this imply (this is the second major question) that the Athenians were deliberately exporting silver (whether as coin or as bullion) or coining for overseas trade in the late 6th and early 5th centuries?

The Athenian silver mines at Laurium were an asset not possessed by most other Greek states.[23] The profit from them early in the 5th century, and the use to which it was put, was undoubtedly crucial to the future development of Athens. But was there an export trade in silver in the period referred to? There is no evidence that the mines were especially productive before about 500: as we have seen, the evidence of the *Wappenmünzen* and the earliest 'owls' (Seltman's Groups H and L) suggests the contrary (Raven 1968, 57–8). If we are to believe Herodotus, Athens's windfall was not large compared with that enjoyed by the Thasians at about the same time. (Herodotus (6.46.3) says that the Thasians enjoyed a total revenue of 200 talents a year from their mines and property on the mainland, 300 talents in a particularly good year.) It was fully utilized by the Athenians themselves almost at once: their new fleet was in action less than four years after the decision to build it. As for the period after the Persian wars, Starr's study of Athenian coinage of the 470s and 460s has led him to suggest that Athens was 'not a wealthy state' at that time (Starr 1970, 81). This assumes that coinage is a reliable indicator of the internal economic position of Athens, and the grounds on which the suggestion is made have been challenged: the quantity of coinage in the 470s and 460s was not insignificant (Kraay 1972, 315–6). Yet it is still true that there is little trace, outside Attica, of the coinage of the period (it is not found at all in western hoards, and is but thinly represented in the Near East (Starr 1970, 84–5; Kraay 1972, 317)) and that a massive injection of funds *from outside* provided the wherewithal for such projects as the Periclean building programme, after 449. Were the early 'owls', then, used abroad by Athenians as a medium of exchange, to facilitate their long-distance trade? There are numerous complications in this hypothesis, but they are certainly worth exploring.

In what sense did Athenian coins arrive at their various destinations as part of *Athenian* trade? Occasionally, more detailed knowledge of the contents of a hoard, and in particular of the dies represented in it, gives a strong hint of direct contact between mint of origin and area of deposition. The best illustration of this, in the late 6th century Ras Shamra hoard from Syria (Thompson *et al* 1973, no 1478; Price & Waggoner 1975, 17), involves not Athenian coins but 31 coins from north Aegean mints: almost every die in the hoard is represented by at least two coins and one die by six (Kraay 1969, 44–5). How can we explain this concentration of die-duplicates, except along the lines suggested by Dr Kraay, that 'this group of coins was not made up locally, but is an undispersed consignment, or part of such a consignment, that had come direct from the north Aegean' (Kraay 1969, 45)? An interesting comparison, this time involving Athenian coins, occurs in an Egyptian hoard from Zagazig (ancient Bubastis, in the Delta), whose date of deposit may be about 450 (Thompson *et al* 1973, no 1645;

Kraay 1975, 147). Among the eight identifiable archaic Athenian coins in the hoard, four belong to group F of the 'owls', issued in the 480s (Price & Waggoner 1975, 61). Three of these four were struck from the same reverse die, which can hardly be fortuitous in view of the rarity of die-links between archaic 'owls' as a whole. Have we the relic of a batch of coins sent more or less direct from Athens to Egypt? In this case the scope for speculation is widened by the long interval between issue and deposition (and during this interval there had been a major Athenian expedition to Egypt). There is a further problem, concerned not so much with numismatics as with the nature of archaic trade. To what extent is there a correlation between the provenance of coins found in archaic hoards and the identity of their carriers? In the case of Egypt, it has been urged that the archaic Greek coins found there are not by themselves proof of a direct commercial route between each coin producer and Egypt (Austin 1970, 37–40; Austin & Vidal-Naquet 1977, 57). In other words, if the coins do indeed represent the residue of payments made by Greeks for purchases in Egypt, the mode of exchange involved was not straightforward 'home-base reciprocity' but rather, 'middleman trading', or perhaps 'down-the-line trade'.[24] In either case, direct Athenian interest in the ultimate destination of the coins would be much reduced or even eliminated.

But 'trade' is not the only factor likely to have promoted the long-distance circulation of coins in the late archaic period. The Persian occupation of much of northern Greece in the years before 480, and the ebb and flow of armies it entailed, must surely have assisted the dispersal of coins from that area, at least to other parts of the Persian empire. The route from Greece to the Levant along the south coast of Asia Minor was used not only for peaceful purposes, but specifically by part of Xerxes's retreating fleet in 480.[25] It is not necessary to assume that there is a single 'true' explanation for the appearance of Athenian coins in a particular area at a particular time. The archaic hoards from Egypt and the Levant have been discussed by Austin (1970, 37–40). For comparison and contrast, I want to look briefly at the finds of archaic Athenian tetradrachms found in the west-central Mediterranean, in particular, in Sicily. These have been described as 'unimpeachable evidence' for Athenian 'enterprise' there before 480 (Mattingly 1969, 220). But we want to try to assess the nature of that 'enterprise', whether commercial or military, official or personal, or whether it existed at all. New discoveries of hoards and continuing analysis of those already known help us to do that.

The hoards in question are the Taranto hoard from south Italy and the Messina, Gela, and Monte Bubbonia hoards from Sicily (see note 18 for reference). Isolated finds of archaic Athenian coins in the west are very rare (Raven 1968, 58, n 1). The nature of the Taranto hoard has been much discussed, but I take it that it is a single find, terminating *c* 500–490,[26] containing around 600 archaic silver coins from all over the Greek world, together with around 6kg of ingots and worked silver. The variety of mints represented in the hoard and the inclusion in it of bullion as well as coins are characteristic of contemporary *eastern* hoards. The comparison is confirmed by the fact that many coins have been cut with a chisel: such test-cuts are also encountered in eastern hoards—the plates of the coins from Asyut in Price & Waggoner (1975) show numerous examples.[27] In the Taranto hoard, coins of eight western mints provide an element not normally found in eastern hoards, but it looks as though the remainder, representing about twenty mints including Athens, reached Taranto by way of the eastern Mediterranean. The Athenian coins are a numerically insignificant proportion of the whole: not more

than eight coins, of which one was a *Wappenmünzen* tetradrachm and five were 'owls' belonging to the earliest group to be issued. In view of the background history of the hoard sketched above, there are no grounds for singling out these coins as in any way reflecting *Athenian* commercial, let alone political, interest in the area of the find. The final collection and deposition of this all-embracing hoard was probably due to the enterprise of an individual, origin unknown, whether merchant, money-changer, or, equally mobile in this as in other periods of Greek history, a soldier. Among the variety of factors that led to the exchange of coins far from their mints of origin, the initiative of an individual or small group should be stressed, and can be illustrated. As just one example, close in time to the closing of the Taranto hoard, we know that a party of Samian adventurers struck coins at Zankle/Messana, in Sicily, before their expulsion from the city in 490/89.[28] We are not told what happened to them after that, but Barron's inference from hoard evidence that they returned east has been dramatically reinforced recently by the presence in the large Asyut hoard of no fewer than fourteen coins of the Samians at Zankle, together with nineteen coins of Samos itself (Barron, 1966, 45; Price & Waggoner 1975, 27; Bicknell 1969, 180. Compare Bicknell 1969, 80, for the suggestion that mercenaries of Hippias took Athenian coins— *Wappenmünzen* and earliest owls—abroad after 510).

In Sicily, the presence of archaic Athenian 'owls' in three hoards offers a more promising hint of some sort of commercial (hardly political) relationship between Athens and Sicily. Two of the hoards (Gela and Monte Bubbonia) were found in an area particularly associated with the production of cereals. At the time of Xerxes's invasion of Greece there was, according to Herodotus (7.158.4), some talk of Gelon's supplying corn to the Greek army; at that time, too, the corn route from the Black Sea to Greece was either threatened or actually controlled by Persia (Herodotus 7.147.2–3; Orlandini 1969, 31). But, once again, we do not know for sure in whose hands these coins came to Sicily. To concentrate on the Athenian element in the hoards is to neglect the puzzling fact that all three contain a coin or coins of Akanthos, and in all three Athens and Akanthos are the only non-Sicilian mints represented. All the Athenian 'owls' in the three Sicilian hoards were struck before 480. The latest of the three, Monte Bubbonia, has a date of deposit of about 465/60 (Kraay 1975, 150); its six Athenian tetradrachms represent a very small proportion of the total of 338 coins, mostly Sicilian (including Rhegium), but including also one tetradrachm of Akanthos. In the inadequately recorded Messina hoard, dated within the period 489–479 (Price & Waggoner 1975, 21) the proportion of Athenian coins is much higher (20+ out of 36+ coins), but few details of them are known. Much the largest of the three hoards, both in the total number of coins and in the number of Athenian coins, is the Gela hoard, now regarded as terminating nearer to 480 than 485 (Price & Waggoner 1975, 20; Kraay 1972, 16). It contained originally well over one thousand coins, of which over 800 were recovered (Jenkins 1970, 150ff). Apart from a handful of tetradrachms of Akanthos, there were two main elements in the hoard: Sicilian and Athenian. In this case, the concentration in a single hoard of 180-odd recently (some very recently) minted Athenian coins may point to a direct importation from Athens, whether by an individual or a group.[29] This hypothesis, and the identity of the importers, is a matter for speculation,[30] but the nature of the differences between the Athenian element in this hoard and that in the Taranto hoard is becoming clearer: it is a question not only of the number of coins, but also of their different histories in circulation before they were hoarded in the west.

The last few paragraphs have been an exercise in the intricacies of interpreting a 'distribution map'. I have asked a number of questions, and have produced not so much answers as a few points that should be borne in mind when formulating answers. To sum up, we have seen in general how detailed analysis of coins in an individual hoard can help us to assess how they reached their ultimate destination. In the particular case of archaic Athenian coins, we can identify a variety of possible reasons for their circulation abroad. I have drawn some attention to individual, personal initiative, as a factor, often in association with military activity, but no single explanation will suffice, and some of those that are offered, such as 'trade', require careful analysis.

During Xerxes's occupation of Athens, the Athenian mint was closed. When coinage resumed, in 478 at the earliest, it was on a smaller scale than before the invasion, until production began to accelerate in the late 450s, and then to outstrip any earlier levels. Starr has set out details of the coinage between 478 and 449, and I have already said a little about its nature and behaviour. Internally, Athenian resources were fully stretched, to recover from the devastation and losses of the Persian wars, and outside sources of precious metals were sought: the mines of Thrace, and booty from marauding expeditions against Persian territory.[31] Externally, this coinage appears from the evidence of hoards to have behaved like most other Greek coins at most times in the archaic and classical periods: on the whole, it did not travel far and was not yet a standard means of exchange in the Aegean, let alone the Mediterranean (Kraay 1964, 76ff). Yet there were important developments in the field of financial management, deriving especially from the formation in 478/7 of the Delian League, and Athens's leadership of it. The involvement of League forces in long summer and winter campaigns in the Aegean and beyond created problems of food-supply, which were met in part by the introduction of cash payments for military, and in particular naval, service (Humphreys 1978, 170ff; Pritchett 1971, 7–14). The funds collected on Delos to pay for this and other League expenses were administered from the start by Athenian officials, the *hellenotamiae*, and in 454 the money was transferred to the Athenian acropolis itself. This move, and the further decision taken perhaps five years later, to spend money contributed by the allies on public building projects in Athens, were of fundamental importance in the history of Athenian public finance. To begin with, there was the sheer magnitude of the sums of money involved. In May 431, at the opening of the Peloponnesian War, there were perhaps 6 000 talents in coined silver stored on the Acropolis, a large proportion consisting of Athenian coins: a decree dated perhaps in the spring of 433 records that 3 000 talents 'in our own coinage' had been brought up to Athena on the acropolis.[32] To give some idea of expenditure in relation to these figures, it has been estimated that between 2 000 and 2 500 talents were spent altogether on the Periclean building programme in Attica, an estimate that may be rather on the low side;[33] in 440 and 439 the treasurers of Athena spent upwards of 1 200 talents on the suppression of the revolt of Samos (Meiggs & Lewis 1969, no 55), and between the summer of 432 and the winter of 430/29, the siege of Potidaea cost more than 2 000 talents (Thucydides 2.70.2; Isocrates 15.113 gives total as 2 400). But in spite of expenses on this scale, the Athenians were able in the 440s and 430s to create and to maintain a substantial reserve, which allowed not only a large increase in the number and range of state payments but also an unprecedented degree of forward financial planning.

Among the host of problems connected with the administration of this reserve and the uses to which it was put, I have chosen to concentrate on one that seemed to me most appropriate to the theme of this conference, and on which there is a good deal of evidence: how were coins actually handled in Athens in the later 5th century? In actual use the coins partook of the character of a 'general-purpose' money —they were employed as a mode of payment, a means of exchange, a standard of value, and as a way of storing wealth.[34] But they were issued originally by the state for a more limited purpose, as payment for materials, and increasingly for service of some kind.

Let us look first at some examples of state payments. Regular payments for military service, whether to hoplites or rowers in the fleet, were a feature of the Periclean period. Military activity has been called the 'central pivot' of the economy of Athens in the 5th century, and it certainly encouraged the circulation of coins both at home and abroad. For payments were not confined to Athenian citizens, and much of the silver earned by allied rowers in the fleet presumably returned to Athens as tribute.[35] In Athens itself, payment for service on juries was probably introduced in the 450s and for attendance at council meetings at about the same time (Rhodes 1972, 13; Buchanan 1962, 14–22). The effect of these measures, in particular the former, on the minting and circulation of obols, must have been dramatic: there were 6 000 jurymen and each was paid two (three after 425) obols for every day on which he sat. Cleon may have been responsible for raising the fee from two to three obols (Rhodes 1972, 13). Aristophanes, in *Wasps* (661–3) produced in 422, reckoned the (maximum) annual expenditure on jury pay at 150 talents, but this would be required only if all 6 000 jurors sat on 300 days at three obols each per day. (In the same play (785–93) one of the characters describes an occasion when the state treasurer, lacking any small change, gave one drachma to a pair of jurors, who then had to make their own arrangements for dividing it: they went to the fish market to get it changed into obols.) The Parthenon was begun in 447, and the surviving building accounts, running from 447/6 to 433/2, record expenditure on purchases of materials, monthly salaries, and day wages (Meiggs & Lewis 1969, no 59). An interesting feature of these accounts is the inheritance by each set of annual commissioners of a group of 74 staters of Lampsacus and 27 staters 1 hekte of Cyzicus. These coins were of electrum, a Lampsacene stater being worth 24 Attic drachmae and a Cyzicene about 27 Attic drachmae in the time of Pericles (Meiggs 1972, 442–3; Bogaert 1963, 85–119), and were obviously not usable in pay packets. At the other end of the scale of value, even the smallest denominations, fractions of an obol, could have served public as much as private needs: for example, the calculation of interest on public loans could involve some very small fractions of an obol (Meiggs & Lewis 1969, no 72).

But coins minted and distributed to individuals by the state acquired a variety of functions as they circulated. In particular, they were often found useful in daily retail trade. We have already seen how our jurymen turned to the market when faced with a problem over change, and in other spheres, too, coins received as pay were employed fairly quickly as a medium of exchange: Thucydides (6.31.3–5), describing the amount of money carried out of Athens with the departing expedition to Sicily in 415, specifically comments that some of it was taken for purposes of exchange. Intense retail market activity in Athens is well documented, in the comic poets for example, and in inscriptions recording prices.[36] The countryside shared in this development,[37] and from 431 the urbanization of the country people, dictated by Pericles's war strategy, brought them face to face with daily trading and markets for staples.[38] Yet there were limitations on the extent to which coinage introduced for a specific purpose could develop as a general purpose currency and replace older methods of exchange (Aristophanes, *Acharnians*, 811ff, 898ff). (I concentrate here on the characteristics of the coinage itself, and cannot develop broader themes—for examples, the inhibiting effect on the circulation of money of social and economic factors such as the ubiquity of slaves and the small scale of business or manufacturing enterprises.) At any one time, especially before 431, a substantial portion of the coinage was out of circulation, stored on the Acropolis. When it did emerge, its flexibility as a medium of payment and exchange was limited. The standard coin, produced in huge numbers, was the tetradrachm. It was a cumbersome business to pay out a large sum in these coins (Demosthenes 27.58), though the use of foreign gold or electrum coins might have reduced the inconvenience. We hear of such coins in the possession of rich individuals, but they were probably as much a means of storing wealth as of spending it.[39] In the sphere of public finance, the treasurers of Athena received electrum coins as tribute (Meiggs 1972, 238–9; Meritt 1932, 8) and payments of Cyzicenes are recorded in their accounts for 418–414 and 408–6.[40] In the middle range of possible denominations, Athens in the later 5th century minted no didrachms and only a restricted number of drachmae.[41] At the lower end of the scale, obols appear to have been relatively plentiful[42] (we have seen why that should be so), and many items necessary for daily survival could be bought for a few obols. Yet even at this level, where their convenience for retail trade was most marked, the use of officially issued coins appears to have encountered practical difficulties. We hear of bronze pieces called *chalkoi* and *kollyboi* in contexts suggesting their use

in transactions involving very small payments. These may have been small bronze tokens, issued by private individuals, 'either as bronze equivalents for the small denominations of silver, or, more probably, as an even smaller fraction' (Price 1968, 100).

This brings me to the last question I want to raise, briefly: that of coinage in metals other than silver. In the period I have chosen to discuss, the coinage of Athens was almost entirely mono-metallic, and it was only when supplies of silver ran out, towards the end of the Peloponnesian War, that alternatives were sought. In 406, the gold plates from seven statues of Victory were melted down for coinage, in denominations ranging from stater to hemiobol. The former was worth 24 silver drachmae, the latter 1 silver drachma.[43] This coinage was intended primarily to meet the costs of materials and services (for example, rowers) outside Attica, and it was complemented by an issue of silverplated bronze coins for internal use.[44] The first bronze coins were probably not minted at Athens until the second half of the 4th century (Kraay 1976, 75), that is, virtually a century later than in several south Italian and Sicilian cities, where bronze coins of several denominations had been used from the third quarter of the 5th century.[45] We know virtually nothing about the reasons that prompted Thurii, for example, soon after its foundation in 444, to issue a copious currency in bronze, alongside its silver coins, but her internal needs were no doubt similar in kind, if not in degree, to those of Athens. The latter was by no means unique in the Greek world in making payments for state service such as the holding of office.[46] But Athens, untypically, possessed in her own territory a steady supply of precious metal. None of the

Historical background

	POLITICAL		FINANCIAL/NUMISMATIC
600			
	594/3	Archonship of Solon	
	c 572	Latest date suggested for Solon's reforms	
	c 560	Peisistratus's first tyranny	
	c 556	Peisistratus's second tyranny	
550			
	546	Peisistratus finally established as tyrant	c 550 First Athenian coinage *(Wappenmünzen)*
	528/7	Death of Peisistratus; Hippias and Hipparchus tyrants	
			c 515 'Owl' coinage begins ('owls' without leaves)
	514	Hipparchus assassinated	
	511/10	Peisistratids expelled	
	508/7	Democratic reforms of Cleisthenes	
500			
	490	Battle of Marathon	
			483/2 Surplus from Laurium silver mines spent on ships
	480	Persians occupy Attica (Battle of Salamis)	480 Coinage interrupted
	478/7	Organization of Delian League	
			c 475 Resumption of coinage ('owls' with leaves)
			c 467 Issue of decadrachms
	462/1	Democratic reforms of Ephialtes	
			454 Delian League funds transferred from Delos to Athens
450			
			434/3 Financial decrees of Callias (ref. to 3 000 talents 'in our own coinage')
	431	Outbreak of Peloponnesian War	
			406 Emergency gold coinage; plated bronze coinage
	404	Surrender of Athens to Sparta	
400			

south Italian and Sicilian cities possessed such a resource, and there the comparative lack of silver for coinage encouraged earlier experimentation with a fiduciary coinage of small bronze pieces.

Acknowledgment

I discussed parts of this paper severally with Mrs S C Humphreys, Dr M J Price, Mr E J P Raven, and Dr P J Rhodes and wish to acknowledge their advice and criticism, together with that of my colleague Dr T J Cadoux, who read a draft of the paper. It should not be assumed that they agree with everything I have written.

Notes

1 Detailed and convincing arguments for a progressive sequence, rather than a side by side (or alternating) arrangement, were set out by Kraay (1956). They replaced an earlier view, expounded by Seltman (1924), that at times in the 6th century there were two mints at Athens, issuing *Wappenmünzen* and 'owls' side by side. A recent attempt to revive a version of the latter view (Cahn 1975) has not to my mind been successful.

2 El *obv* types: owl, wheel, bull's head; *rev*: punch-mark. There are two denominations, one (with owl and wheel) weighing between 1.31 and 1.44g, the other (with bull's head) 0.67g: cf Seltman 1924, 80–1, catalogue nos 306–10 (p 193), and pl XIV, P251A199 to P255A203.

3 Both didrachms and smaller denominations share a common fabric and weight standard (Euboic–Attic); among the didrachms there are occasional reverse die-links between different obverse dies.

4 In addition to the points made by Kraay (1976, 57–8), note that many of the symbols on *Wappenmünzen* (wheel, astragalos, bull's head, amphora) are found also on Athenian bronze weights, one of the earliest of which (with astragalos) is dated *c* 500 BC (Lang & Crosby 1964, 6, 25).

5 For details and illustrations of the technical development sketched here, see Kraay 1956, 45–6 and pl XIII, 6 (didrachm with lion's head in incuse square), 7 (tetradrachm with *rev* lion's head in incuse square, surrounded by wide flattened area of metal), 8 (early 'owl' with similar *rev* technique).

6 Seltman's division into lettered groups is still employed as the basis for discussion: the groups showing *obv* Athena without leaves are H, L, M, Gi, Gii, F, C, E. Price & Waggoner (1975) assign Roman numerals to these groups, as follows: II(H), III(L), IV(M,G), V(F,C), VI(E).

7 W P Wallace's arguments (1962, 23–42, esp 23–35), supporting Seltman's view that the change took place in 490, were rejected by Kraay (1962, 417–23) in favour of a date near 480. The latter was supported by Starr (1970, 3–7, 16–19), whose conclusions were worked out in relation not only to the preceding issues but to the succeeding issues as well: they do not depend on a doubtful association of new elements in the types (*obv* olive leaves on helmet; *rev* crescent) with a victory over the Persians.

8 In the reconstruction that follows in the text, the arguments from hoard evidence outweigh both literary evidence for Athenian coinage in Solon's time (Aristotle, *AP*, 10), and also the view that the dies of many archaic owls were engraved in a style more appropriate to the first half of the 6th century than to any other period (Ashmole 1938, 17–22; Cahn 1946, 133–43). Arguments from the hoard evidence (Kraay 1956, 48–52) have been strengthened by recent discoveries (see now Kraay 1975; Price & Waggoner 1975, 56–68). 'Owls' start to appear in hoards only after 500, and to suppose that some of them were minted in the first half of the 6th century (in some cases up to a hundred years before their deposition) requires some unnecessarily complicated and unlikely explanations of the hoard evidence. Cahn's attempt (1946, 83–4) to use the evidence of the state of wear of coins in the Gela hoard (*IGCH* 2066) to support his earlier dating of the 'owls' fails, because '. . . the degree of wear varies considerably within each of the main [Athenian] groups represented in the hoard . . .', so that 'it is difficult . . . to see any regular pattern in the wear data for the Athenian coins in this hoard which would be admissable as evidence either for or against any particular arrangement of Athenian coinage . . .' (Jenkins 1970, 151).

9 Price & Waggoner 1975, 65, dating the reforms in 506. For discussion of the date, and of the order of events in 508/7, see Hignett 1952, 124–8, 331–6.

10 Cf the remark of Price & Waggoner (1975, 65), in the context of a discussion of the source of the silver from which the earliest 'owls' were minted, that '. . . the erratic nature of the style of group II [the earliest] of the owls may well suggest that it does not represent continuous striking of mined silver, but more sporadic minting as silver became available.'

11 So Raven (1968, 58). An anecdote in ps-Aristotle, *Economica* ii, 1347a, ascribes to Hippias a reform of Athenian coinage involving the striking of a new χαρατήρ. The word χαρατήρ here should mean 'type', and the passage may preserve a record of the introduction of the 'owls' (Williams 1966, 12–3), but the corrupt text admits of more

than one interpretation. A unique obol (Seltman 1924, 76 and pl XXII, Π, with *obv* helmeted head of Athena, *rev* owl, ear of corn, HIΓ, may have been issued by Hippias (or Hipparchus). If it was, then it could be regarded as evidence for an owl coinage before 510, even if it was itself struck after that date, say, by Hippias in exile. But the issuing authority, place of minting, and date of the coin are all uncertain, and the stylistic relationship between the *obv* head and heads on Group H of the archaic tetradrachms is not universally accepted. (Bicknell (1969, 176) accepts it; Price & Waggoner (1975, 132, n 92) do not.)

12 For this and other figures in the remainder of the paragraph, see Hopper 1968, 38. Comparably accurate and up to date figures for other contemporary mints are hard to come by. The standard study of the extensive 6th century coinage of Corinth is based on 146 coins, minted from 66 *obv* dies and 67 *rev* dies (Ravel 1936). Price & Waggoner (1975, 76–9) have suggested a span of approximately 50 years (550–500) for these coins.

13 For details of the building projects of Peisistratus and his sons, see Boersma 1970, 11–27. The ambitious programme of the sons contrasts with the modest aim and achievement of the father (*op cit*, 26–7); note especially their extensive building programme on the Acropolis and the vigorous promotion of Athena as Attica's representative deity (*op cit*, 21), an eminently suitable context for the introduction of the 'owl' coinage.

14 Yalouris 1950, 52–4. Cf Raven's suggestion reported by Kraay (1956, 65, n 1) that 'the type [of the *Wappenmünzen*] was changed every four years at the Greater Panathenaea'. At a much later date, in the 2nd and 1st centuries BC, and again in the Roman imperial period, many symbols on Athenian coins are without question agonistic, some specifically Panathenaic (Thompson 1942, 214–17). For an example of the spending on a festival of money acquired as booty, see Diodoros Siculus, 12.70.5 (the Thebans after the battle of Delium, 424).

15 Herodotus 5.77.1–3. The proceeds from the Boeotians amounted to 23¼ talents. One-tenth of the total derived from Boeotians *and* Chalcidians was dedicated on the Acropolis in the form of a bronze quadriga. If, say, 1 000 prisoners had been ransomed in all, the treasury would have received about 30 talents.

16 At the turn of the century, Athens had 50 ships (Herodotus 6.89); in 489, Miltiades took 70 ships to Paros (*ibid* 6.132); when the Greeks confronted the Persians at Salamis, Athens contributed 180 out of an allied force of 378 ships (*ibid* 8.44.1,48).

17 On the sustained Athenian interest in the coast of Thrace and Macedon in the 6th and 5th centuries, see Austin & Vidal-Naquet 1977, 117–8. Athenian coins rarely travelled north before the Hellenistic period (Thompson *et al* 1973, 56).

18 In Thompson *et al* 1973 (their nos quoted): Italy: 1874 (Taranto); Sicily: 2065 (Messina), 2066 (Gela), 2071 (Monte Bubbonia); Egypt: 1638 (Delta), 1646 (Fayum), 1640 (Benha), 1644 (Asyut), 1645 (Zagazig); Levant: 1479 (Dieble), 1482 (Jordan).

19 Thompson *et al* 1973, 153 and nos 1172 (Chios), 1173 (Cos), 1177 (S. Asia Minor) contain archaic 'owls'.

20 On the political and religious context before 511/10, see note 13. If introduced after 510, the 'owls' might be regarded as a 'symbol of the democracy itself and freedom from tyranny' (Price & Waggoner 1974, 65).

21 Cf the cogent remarks of Gauthier (1975, 168–9). Gauthier does not wish to underestimate the probable function of the ethnic as an aid to identification in international commerce, but questions whether that was the initial reason for its inscription on coins. He points out that the inclusion of such a feature was not necessary to ensure the wide circulation of coins (cf the coinages of Thasos and Aegina), and compares the practice on bronze coins, where the inclusion of an ethnic could not have been designed to secure their wider circulation.

22 The larger coin, the tetradrachm, had strictly speaking been introduced before the other two changes—probably not long before, but the interval does help to smooth the transition from *Wappenmünzen* to 'owls'.

23 The list of city states favoured in this way is brief: Thasos, a few other cities in Thrace, Siphnos, and Athens. Some cities in Asia Minor had access to electrum. Will 1975, 97–8.

24 For a discussion of some different modes of exchange, introducing the terms used here, see Renfrew 1975, 41–6.

25 Compare Robinson (1961, 117) on a hoard deposited about 480 (Thompson *et al* 1973, no 1177), on the south coast of Anatolia, not far from the Pamphylian–Cilician border, 'on the main sea route followed by Persian fleets to and from the West.'

26 Price & Waggoner 1975, 19. The date is based on the presence in the hoard of three medium incuse coins of Metapontum, but the group of imported coins, including the Athenian, may have 'an appreciably earlier date' (Kraay 1977, 195).

27 Two contemporary Egyptian hoards contain coins from different areas, and other silver objects (references are to Thompson *et al* 1973): Mit Rahineh (1636); Demanhur (1637). Cf also the contents of two slightly later hoards, also from Egypt: Asyut, *c* 475 (1644); Zagazig, after 470 (1645). The Ras Shamra hoard, from Syria (1478; end of 6th century), contained coins, partially melted coins, and silver lumps. For chisel cuts on many coins in the taranto hoard, see Babelon 1912, 4ff.

28 For discussion of this date, see Barron 1966, 40–3. A fraction marked Z has been reported at Oxford (*Ashmolean Museum Report to the Visitors* 1969–70, 39), and if this letter is an addition to the previously known sequence of five issues, the Samians stayed on another year, leaving in 489/8.

29 There are very few (4+) from Groups H and L (6th century), 38 from Group M, 96 from Group G (both *c* 500/490–*c* 482), and 31 from Group C (*c* 482–480). (Figures from Kraay 1975, 152; dates from Price & Waggoner 1975, 57–61).

30 Price & Waggoner (1975, 20) wonder whether the Athenian coins 'belonged originally to one of the Athenian families which fled from the city in the face of the Persian advance in 480'. Herodotus (8.41.1) gives no hint of such a distant destination, and mentions only Troezen, Aegina, and Salamis.

31 Thracian mines: Thucydides 1.100.2; booty: Thucydides 1.96.1. Booty from the battle of Eurymedon may have been the source of the silver for a unique Athenian issue of decadrachms, in the mid 460s (Starr 1970, 38–42). The reasons for the issue of such a large denomination are not clear.

32 According to the 'book texts' of Thucydides 2.13.3, Pericles spoke of 6 000 talents on the acropolis in May 431; according to a quotation of Thucydides 2.13.3 preserved in the scholia to Aristophanes, *Plutus* 1193, Pericles said that 6 000 talents had been accumulated for several years, and Thucydides comments that at the time Pericles spoke, the figure was actually 5 700 talents: for discussion, see Meritt *et al* 1950, 118–32. For 3 000 talents in 433, see Meiggs & Lewis 1969, no 58.

33 Burford 1965, 25. Estimates for individual projects include 470 talents for the Parthenon (cf Stanier 1953, 68–76), *c* 200 talents for the Propylaea, 50 talents for the Hephaisteion, 40–50 talents for the temple of Ares in Athens, and 40–50 talents for the temple of Poseidon at Sounion. However, all such calculations are uncertain. Meiggs & Lewis (1969, 165) suggest between 700 and 800 talents for the Parthenon, and regard 2 000 talents as 'a credible figure' for the combined cost of the Parthenon, the cult-statue, and the Propylaea.

34 The three main uses of money are as payment, means of exchange, and standard; it may also be used as a means of storing wealth. The term 'general-purpose money' has been applied to any item which serves all three major uses: Polanyi (1957, 264–6). For further discussion and references, cf Grierson 1977, 14–19.

35 Sources and references on military pay are collected by Kendrick Pritchett (1971, 7–12). On the role of military activity in the Athenian economy, see Humphreys 1978, 169ff and, in general, Bolkestein (1958, 145). 'This waging of war was the most extensive trade known in Greece, ... the state, the political organization of the citizens, procured a livelihood to its citizens by waging war'.

36 References in comedy are collected and discussed by Ehrenberg (1951, 219–52); cf also Burelli 1973, 767–86. For discussion of epigraphic evidence for prices, see Amyx 1958, 275–310. Another source of information, trademarks on Greek vases, is discussed by Johnston (1974, 138–52).

37 There is more work to be done on the literary and other evidence on this topic. Contrast the respective attitudes of Cimon and Pericles to the disposal of the produce of their estates: the former generous with gifts of food, allowing any who wished to gather the fruits of his unenclosed estates (Aristotle, *AP*, 27.3–4; cf Plutarch, *Pericles* 9.2), the latter practising a strict *oikonomia*, in which all the annual produce was sold in bulk, and all the necessities were bought in the market (Plutarch, *Pericles* 16.3–6). But cf, in the prologue of Aristophanes's *Acharnians*, the nostalgia of a countryman for his deme, where the word 'buy' is unknown (vv 33–6). The economic role of the sanctuaries of Attica would repay investigation: festivals, new building, lending activities (cf the accounts of Nemesis at Rhamnous, *c* 450–40: Meiggs & Lewis 1969, no 53).

38 At the opening of the Peloponnesian War, the country people of Attica, on Pericles's advice, brought their families and movable property inside the walls of Athens: Thucydides 2.14.

39 30 Cyzicenes possessed by Diodotus in 409: Lysias 32.5, 6, 15; 400 Cyzicenes and 100 darics possessed by Lysias himself in 404: Lysias 12.11. These coins were probably kept at home: cf Bogaert 1968, 368.

40 *IG²* I.302.13,57,65; *IG²* I.301.93ff, 120ff; cf Ferguson 1932: 23. For a list of references to Cyzicenes in Athenian (and Delphic) treasuries, see Bogaert 1963, 85, n 2.

41 Didrachms were minted in the 5th century only between the late 470s and the early 450s: Starr, Groups II–IV inclusive. In the coinage after 480, Starr (1970, 21) assigned 'considerable numbers' of drachmae to his Group II, and also to Groups III and IV; in Group V, on the other hand, there are 'remarkably few' drachmae (1970, 56). This takes us down to about the middle of the century; after that, 'Drachmas were issued in restricted numbers' (1970, 70).

42 In Starr's Groups V, 'obols are relatively more numerous ... than in any [Group] previously' (Starr 1970, 56); obols (and hemiobols) are 'relatively more numerous' after *c* 450 (1970, 70–1).

43 Other denominations, with their silver equivalents, were: drachma (12 drachmae), triobol (6), diobol (4), and obol (2). The gold coinage is referred to as 'new' at v 720 of Aristophane's *Frogs*, produced in late January 405. On problems connected with it (dating, function, amount of metal minted, etc), see Robinson 1960, 8–13; Thompson 1965, 159–74; 1966, 337–43; 1970, 1–6.

44 This has been the commonly held view: see Robinson 1960, 8–12; Thompson 1966, 337–43; Kraay 1976, 69–70. It was challenged by Giovannini (1975, 185–90); a reply has been published (Kroll 1976, 329–41).

45 These coinages were the subject of the sixth convegno organized (17–22 April 1977) by the Centro Internazionale di Studi Numismatici, Naples ('L'inizio della monetazione di bronzo in Sicilia e nella Magna Grecia', *Atti*, Rome, 1979).

46 Evidence for political pay outside Athens has been collected by de Ste Croix (1975, 48–52). There is explicit evidence for it at Rhodes and Iasus (in Caria), and it would be interesting to explore its possible repercussions in the surviving coinage of these cities.

Bibliography

Allen, D F, 1976 Wealth, money and coinage in a Celtic society, in Megaw, J V S (ed), *To illustrate the monuments: essays on archaeology presented to Stuart Piggott* 200–8

Amyx, D A, 1958 The attic stelai: Part III Vases and other containers; IX Price of containers, *Hesperia* 27, 275–310

Ashmole, B, 1938 The relation between coins and sculpture, in Allan, J, Mattingly, H, and Robinson, E S G, *Trans Int Numis Congress* (London), 17–22 (organized and held in London by the Royal Numismatic Society 30 June–3 July 1936)

Austin, M M, 1970 Greece and Egypt in the Archaic Age, *Proc Cambridge Phil Soc*, Supplement No 2

Austin, M M & Vidal-Naquet, P, 1977 *Economic and social history of ancient Greece: an introduction*

Babelon, J, 1912 Trouvaille de Tarente, *Revue Numis*, 16, 14 ser, 1–40

Barron, J P, 1966 *The silver coins of Samos*

Bicknell, P J, 1969 The dates of the Archaic owls of Athens belonging to Seltman's Groups H and L, *Antiq Class*, 38, 175–80

Boersma, J S, 1970 *Athenian building policy from 561/0 to 405/4 BC*

Bogaert, R, 1963 Le cours du statère de Cyzique aux Vᵉ et IVᵉ Siècles avant J-C, *Antiq Class*, 32, 85–119

Bogaert, R, 1968 *Banques et banquiers dans les cités grecques*

Bolkestein, H, 1958 *Economic life in Greece's Golden Age* (revised and annotated by E J Jonkers)

Buchanan, J J, 1962 *Theorika: a study of monetary distributions to the Athenian citizenry during the fifth century BC*

Burelli, L, 1973 Metafore monetali e provvedimenti finanziari in Aristofane, *Annali della Scuola Normale di Pisa*, 3, 3, 767–86

Burford, A M, 1965 The economics of Greek temple building, *Proc Cambridge Phil Soc*, 191, n ser 2, 21–34

Cahn, H A, 1946 Zur frühattischen Münzprägung, *Mus Helveticum*, 3, 133–43

Cahn, H A, 1975 *Kleine Schriften zur Münzkunde und Archäologie*

Ehrenberg, V, 1951 *The people of Aristophanes*

Ferguson, W S, 1932 *The treasurers of Athena*

Finley, M I, 1973 *The ancient economy*

Gauthier, Ph, 1975 Légendes monétaires grecques, in Dentzer, J-M, Gauthier, Ph, & Hackens, T (eds), *Numismatique Antique: problèmes et méthodes*, 165–79

Giovannini, A, 1975 Athenian currency in the late fifth and early fourth century BC, *Greek, Roman Byzantine Stud*, 16, 185–95

Grierson, P, 1959 Commerce in the Dark Ages: a critique of the evidence, *Trans Roy Hist Soc*, 9, 123–40

Grierson, P, 1961 La fonction sociale de la monnaie en Angleterre aux VIIᵉ–VIIIᵉ siècles, in *Moneta e scambi nell'alto medioevo*, 341–62 (Settimane di Studio del Centro Italiano di Studi sull'alto Medioevo, VIII, 21–7 aprile 1960)

Grierson, P, 1977 *The origins of money* (The Creighton Lecture in History 1970)

Hignett, C, 1952 *A history of the Athenian constitution*

Hopper, R J, 1960 A note on Aristophanes, Lysistrata 665–70, *Class Quart*, 10, n ser, 242–7

Hopper, R J, 1968 Observations on the *Wappenmünzen*, in Kraay, C M, & Jenkins, G K (eds), *Essays in Greek coinage presented to Stanley Robinson*, 16–39

Humphreys, S C, 1978 *Anthropology and the Greeks*

Jenkins, G K, 1970 *The coinage of Gela*

Johnston, A W, 1974 Trademarks on Greek vases, *Greece and Rome*, 21, 138–52

Kraay, C M, 1956 The archaic owls of Athens: classification and chronology, *Numis Chron*, 16, 43–68

Kraay, C M, 1962 The early coinage of Athens: a reply, *ibid*, 2, 7 ser, 417–23

Kraay, C M, 1964 Hoards, small change and the origin of coinage, *J Hellenic Stud*, 84, 76–91

Kraay, C M, 1969 *Greek coins and history*

Kraay, C M, 1972 The Demareteion reconsidered: a reply, *Numis Chron*, 12, 7 ser, 13–24

Kraay, C M, 1975 Archaic owls of Athens: new evidence for chronology, *Miscellanea Graeca*, 1, 145–57

Kraay, C M, 1976 *Archaic and classical Greek coins*

Kraay, C M, 1977 The Asyut hoard: some comments on chronology, *Numis Chron*, **17,** 7 ser, 189–98

Kroll, J H, 1976 Aristophanes' πουηεά χαλκια: a reply, *Greek, Roman Byzantine Stud*, **17,** 329–41

Labarbe, J, 1957 *La loi navale de Thémistocle*

Lang, M, & Crosby, M, 1964 *The Athenian Agora*, **10,** *Weights, measures and tokens*

Mattingly, H B, 1969 Athens and the Western Greeks: *c* 500–413 BC, in *La circolazione della moneta ateniese in Sicilia e in Magna Grecia* (Atti del 1° convegno del Centro Internazionale di Studi Numismatici, Napoli, 5–8 aprile 1967), 201–21

Meiggs, R, 1972 *The Athenian empire*

Meiggs, R, & Lewis D, 1969 *A selection of Greek historical inscriptions*

Meritt, B D, 1932 *Athenian financial documents of the fifth century*

Meritt, B D, Wade-Gery, H T, & McGregor, M F, 1950 *The Athenian tribute lists*, **3**

Orlandini, P, 1969 in *La circolazione della moneta ateniese in Sicilia e in Magna Grecia* (Atti del 1° convegno del Centro Internazionale di Studi Numismatici, Napoli, 5–8 aprile 1967), 30–1

Parke, H W, 1933 *Greek mercenary soldiers*

Polanyi, K, 1957 The economy as instituted process, in Polanyi, K, Arensberg, C M, & Pearson, H W (eds), *Trade and market in the early empires*

Price, M J, 1968 Early Greek bronze coinage in Kraay, C M, & Jenkins, G K (eds), *Essays in Greek coinage presented to Stanley Robinson*, 90–104

Price, M J, & Waggoner, N, 1975 *Archaic Greek silver coinage: the 'Asyut' hoard*

Pritchett, W P, 1971 *Ancient Greek military practices*, **1**

Ravel, O E, 1936 *Les poulains de Corinthe*, **1**

Raven, E J P, 1968 Problems of the earliest owls of Athens, in Kraay, C M, & Jenkins, G K (eds), *Essays in Greek coinage presented to Stanley Robinson*, 40–58

Renfrew, C, 1975 Trade as action at a distance: questions of integration and communication, in Sabloff, J A, & Lamberg-Karlovsky, C C, *Ancient civilization and trade*

Rhodes, P J, 1972 *The Athenian boule*

Robinson, E S G, 1960 Some problems in the later fifth century coinage of Athens, *Amer Numis Soc Mus Notes*, **9,** 1–15

Robinson, E S G, 1961 A hoard of archaic Greek coins from Anatolia, *Numis Chron*, **1,** 7 ser, 107–17

Ste Croix, G E M de, 1975 Political pay outside Athens, *Class Quart*, **25,** n ser, 48–52

Seltman, C, 1924 *Athens, its history and coinage*

Stanier, R J, 1953 The cost of the Parthenon, *J Hellenic Stud*, **73,** 68–76

Starr, C G, 1970 *Athenian coinage, 480–449 BC*

Thompson, M, 1942 Coins for the Eleusinia, *Hesperia*, **11,** 213–29

Thompson, M, Mørkholm, O, & Kraay, C M (eds), 1973 *An inventory of Greek coin hoards*

Thompson, W E, 1965 The date of Athenian gold coinage, *Amer J Philology*, **86,** 159–74

Thompson, W E, 1966 The function of the emergency coinages of the Peloponnesian War, *Mnemosyne*, **19,** 337–433

Thompson, W E, 1970 The golden nikai and the coinage of Athens, *Numis Chron*, **10,** 7 ser, 1–6

Wallace, M B, 1974 Herodotos and Euboia, *Phoenix*, **28,** 22–44

Wallace, W P, 1962 The early coinages of Athens and Euboia, *Numis Chron*, **2,** 7 ser, 23–42

Will, Ed, 1975 Les sources des métaux monnayés dans le monde grec, in Dentzer, J-M, Gauthier, Ph, & Hackens, T (eds), *Numismatique antique: problèmes et méthodes*, 97–102

Williams, R T, 1966 The 'owls' and Hippias, *Numis Chron*, **6,** 7 ser, 9–13

Yalouris, N, 1950 Athena als Herrin der Pferde, *Mus Helveticum*, **7,** 65–101

The use of coinage in Central Gaul before the Roman conquest of 51 BC is very distinctive and, owing to the existence of comparatively full documentary evidence, it is possible to outline the likely connections between the development of the coinage in the 1st century BC and that of Central Gaulish political formations (Nash 1978a; forthcoming).

Central Gaulish coinages of the 1st century have a number of characteristics which distinguish them from earlier issues of the area. Each of the major 1st century *civitates* appears to have had at least one precious metal coinage with types peculiar to itself and often owing little to earlier issues. Thus, for instance, ABVDOS group gold (Nash 1978a.202ff) follows a series of different gold staters of Philip II type (*ibid*, 94ff), and Bituriges silver with sword (*ibid*, 210ff) is not related in type to earlier west Berry silver (*ibid*, 41ff). In addition, there were pronounced differences in weight standards between the coinages of different *civitates*, whilst gold coinages also differed in fineness from one *civitas* to another.[1] Both silver and gold coinages were issued by some *civitates*. In the case of the Arverni, the principal gold stater coinage was accompanied by silver and sometimes bronze denominations with the same types, suggesting that there was a trimetallic coinage (Nash 1978a, 145ff); the gold staters of the Bituriges were accompanied by bronze but not silver fractions (Nash 1978a, 202ff, 207, 210ff). More commonly, however, two or more precious metal coinages in one *civitas* were not apparently related to one another in type, sometimes show different geographical distribution, and were very likely struck from different centres. This raises some important issues about the authorship of Central Gaulish coinage in the 1st century BC.

It is undoubtedly the case that the main gold stater series found in Auvergne (Fig 2) was the official gold coinage of the central government of the 1st century Arvernian *civitas*: it is almost all found in the Limagne valley within range of their largest and most important settlements, including

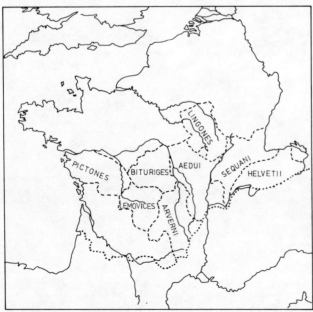

Fig 1 Central Gaulish civitates

Gergovia, and one type carries the name of the Arvernian Vercingetorix who was prominent in the Gaulish resistance to the Roman conquest in 52–51 BC (Caesar *BG* 7.4.3). The geographical situation of the Arverni clearly contributed to the emergence of a single dominant political centre in this area: the complex of settlements in the region of Gergovia was established in the only large fertile valley in Arvernian territory, and could control traffic on the river Allier, while the rest of Arvernian territory was largely granitic and mountainous. For this reason the principal Arvernian coinage is confined in distribution almost exclusively to the region of the Limagne valley, not scattered over the larger part of their territory. No coinage can be expected to spread itself evenly over a political territory, because the distribution of coinage depends on the pattern of settlement and land use of the society using it, a fact which makes the use of distribution patterns of Celtic coinage to establish the probable territories of Celtic peoples a very unreliable tool. Subdivisions within the main Arvernian coinage are difficult to establish and may not represent different authorship, but there are several small issues of silver which are unrelated to it, but probably of Massif Central origin, which are not of the same origin as the principal issues (Nash 1978a, 170ff, 145). It is probable therefore that more than one political authority was producing precious metal coins within Arvernian territory in the 1st century, some of them outside the main complex of settlements.

One obvious way to attempt to establish difference in authorship is to distinguish coin types and styles from one another, but unfortunately this is not necessarily a reliable method, as the wide range of types struck by the earliest Athenian mint, the *Wappenmünzen*, and the coinage of republican Rome will demonstrate. There is as yet no reliable way to distinguish between a change in artist within one Celtic mint and a difference in mint of origin in many cases. The gold and silver coinage of the Arverni and the silver coinage of the Bituriges Cubi raise the problem in an acute form (Nash 1978, 138ff, 210ff). The Arvernian stater coinage had at least 24 varieties, accompanied by many silver types, while Biturigan sword group silver has sixteen different symbol combinations. Yet in each case the different varieties are found thoroughly mixed in hoards, while two dies for different varieties of Biturigan silver coin were found on the Arvernian settlement of Puy de Corent, where they were presumably abandoned by the Biturigan military contingent after the siege of Gergovia in 51 BC (Nash 1978a, 201, 213; Blanchet 1905, 32, 413). Close similarity in style and absolute conformity in weight suggests a common origin for each category of these coinages, and mixture in hoards and overlapping distribution patterns within Arvernian or Biturigan territory respectively suggest equal monetary validity for all the varieties of each coinage within their own *civitates*. The significance of the different types is therefore uncertain, but in these two cases it is not unreasonable to suggest that the different types represent different moneyers striking state bullion, or perhaps individual nobles called upon to provide coinages from their own resources, struck to the legal *civitas* standard, but who in return for their enforced generosity retained the right to mark their coin with individual types. In the political environment of wealthy oligarchies characteristic of the 1st century Central Gaulish *civitates*, the latter hypothesis might seem attractive, if unproven.

In other cases, difference in coin metal and type may be regarded as a result of separate authorship within the *civitas*. Poitou base gold and silver coins are found with overlapping though not coextensive distributions, but gold and silver are seldom found significantly mixed in pre-conquest hoards (Fig 3).[2] The two coinages are also quite separate in metal and type. The base gold series is markedly Armorican in fabric, weight, and style, while the silver is on its own idiosyncratic weight standard and is derived in type from one of several late 2nd century silver coinages of western Berry on the eastern border of Poitou, beyond the river Vienne. The distribution of Poitou silver clusters near Poitiers and Niort, on the Iron Age coastline; the gold has a distribution extending significantly further north as far as the right bank of the Loire and occasionally into Armorica. These coinages were contemporary, as is shown by hoards and site finds, but it is difficult to believe that they were both official coinages of the main *civitas* authority. In that case they would have had to have been linked in a formal bimetallic system as were Arvernian gold and silver. But the latter shared types between the different denominations to mark their connection, instead of being sharply differentiated. It is therefore a likely hypothesis that Poitou gold and silver were struck by different political authorities, each with a separate history and perhaps different outside connections (Colbert de Beaulieu 1971).

The likelihood that precious metal coinages were struck at different centres within a 1st century *civitas* is strongest in the case of the Bituriges Cubi (Fig 4). Here the gold stater coinage is mostly confined within the *civitas* borders, while the silver coinage is found in Berry and neighbouring Poitou (Nash 1978a, 202ff, 210ff). The two coinages are different in type and not exactly coextensive in distribution:

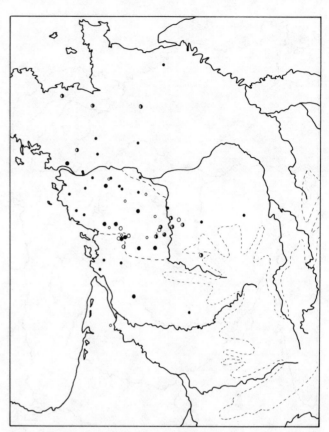

Fig 3 Pictones coinage: ● ● *gold hoards and stray finds;* ◑ *gold coins in mixed hoard;* ○ ○ *silver hoards and stray finds*

the silver coinage probably travelled far in the Caesarian war and the early conquest period, and it is now impossible to distinguish pre- from post-conquest circulation patterns. It is notable, however, that the silver coinage is found more to the west of Biturigan territory than the gold, and that some fine early specimens have been found on the major settlement of Argentomagus (St Marcel, Indre), whose name encapsulates the root *Argent*– (silver) and stands near a source of silver ore (Cothenet 1968). Gold coinage, and its fractional bronze, has a more south-westerly distribution in the *civitas;* both have been found on the site of Levroux and bronze in some quantity in Bourges itself, the ancient 'capital'.

It is possible, though not proven, that the gold stater coinage was that of the central government at Avaricum (Bourges), while the silver was produced at Argentomagus. There were four major defended settlements within the territory of the Bituriges Cubi, and it is not unlikely that each was the central settlement of a *pagus* or major province of the *civitas*. There is documentary evidence to suggest that in the 1st century the *pagi* of each *civitas* retained a considerable degree of administrative autonomy from the central *civitas* government, for instance in providing their own military levy (Nash 1978b). Given that armies were probably the single largest item of state expenditure, it is not improbable that a *pagus* with the resources to pay for its own levy was obliged to do so; this would account for precious metal coinages struck by different mints within a *civitas* such as the Pictones or Bituriges Cubi.[3]

In contrast to the sometimes very diffuse distribution pattern of early Celtic coinages, the geographical distribution of each 1st century Central Gaulish precious metal coinage was relatively limited, with the exception of silver coinages on the weight standard of the Roman quinarius at *c* 1.80–1.90g. The latter were used widely during the

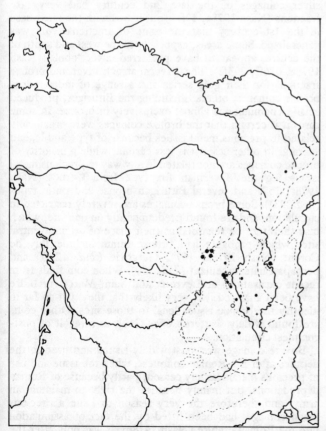

Fig 2 Auvergne coinage: ● ● *Arvernian gold staters, hoard and stray find;* ○ ○ *Arvernian silver coins in hoard and stray find;* + *other Auvergne silver type*

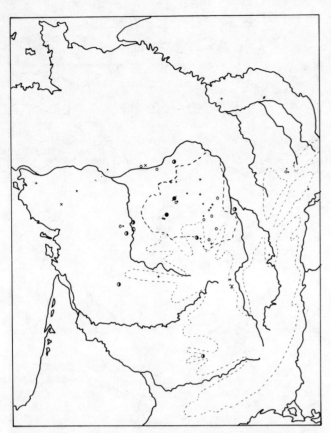

Fig 4 Bituriges coinage: ○ ○ *gold coins, hoard and stray find;* ● ● *silver coins, hoard and stray find;* ◐ *silver coins in mixed hoard;* ◖ *Bituriges silver and gold hoard;* + × *ABVDOS group bronze coins, stray finds and in hoard;* ✕ *silver coin dies*

campaigns of the Caesarian war, and continued in use afterwards well beyond their original source, with the result that in a few cases it is now difficult to determine their place of origin. But given that we have independent knowledge of the territorial boundaries of the 1st century Central Gaulish *civitates*, it is evident that in general all gold and most silver coinages were restricted in circulation to their home territories, a circumstance of some political importance.

The chronology of the late coinages is of considerable importance if they are to be related to political developments. Late coinage was frequently hoarded, but is seldom found in hoards together with specimens of earlier coinages, even when these were used in the same area. The clearest examples are provided by the Aedui and Bituriges, where in the former case Chenôves-type gold is never found with 1st century silver, while Biturigan gold is not hoarded with specimens of earlier gold issues (Nash 1978a, 72, 202f). The late precious metal coinages were therefore significantly later than the earlier coinages. The length of time lapses between coinage phases is unknown; it is possible that coinage issue was a very rare phenomenon before the 1st century, with long periods when old coins may have been used but none struck. The fact that only one certain stray find of 2nd century silver coins has been made in Berry, whereas several large hoards are known (Nash 1978a, 42) might suggest that even the use of coin, except for wealth storage, was not always very widespread.

A 1st century date for the late phase of coinage is certain on the basis of the chronology of silver hoards containing Roman coins, the development of coin types from dated prototypes, the rare inclusion of names of known 1st century nobles on some issues, and from the composition of finds from the mass grave of Gaulish dead at the siege of Alesia in 51 BC. 449 Gaulish and 134 Roman coins were

found there, and the Gaulish coins provide a valuable guide to issues in use in the 50s in Central and some remoter areas of Gaul (Colbert de Beaulieu 1955). Most important, however, is the fact that it is, with rare exceptions, only coins of the late phase which are found on sites occupied in the 1st century BC. No major defended site, even an early and important one such as Argentomagus or Levroux, has yielded coins of the early phases, although later coinage in precious metal as well as bronze is abundant on them, and Levroux and Argentomagus, at least, stood within one of the areas of Central Gaul which had a rich early coinage. It is therefore to be inferred that the earlier coinages had gone out of use before the intensive settlement of the defended sites. There is some disagreement about the original date of their settlement but it may be argued that they were in existence not later than the first years of the 1st century BC, if not somewhat earlier. *Murus gallicus* construction may now be dated well before the Caesarian war (Büchsenschütz & Ralston 1975), and the major settlements of the Bituriges all had *murus gallicus* defences. In some cases the settlement of the sites preceded the construction of the defences, thus pushing its date further back still (eg Châteaumeillant: Nash 1978a, 182, or Levroux: *ibid*, 192).

No 1st century mint has been identified beyond doubt on archaeological grounds in Central Gaul, but it is probable that precious metal, as well as bronze, coins were normally struck at major administrative centres—usually defended settlements. For reasons already outlined, it is likely that the authority responsible for issuing the coinage was either the central government or a major section of the state responsible for financing an army or supporting some other important state function.

Finally, one of the most important new developments in the late phase coinages was the appearance for the first time of bronze coinage and small silver fractions. A few of the silver coinages of the late 2nd century had very rare fractions (Nash 1978a, 49ff), but it was with the late phase in the 1st century that the issue of fractional coin was generalized. Some areas, especially to the west and south of the centre, appear to have preferred silver 'obols' (Nash 1978a, 626ff, 293ff). The Arverni struck silver and bronze fractions for their gold series and a range of independent bronze coinages; others, including the Bituriges, produced small denominations almost exclusively in bronze. In some cases it is certain that the bronze coinages were organically related to precious metal issues because of type and legend sharing. In other cases it is less certain, while a majority of bronze coinages are not related in any way to precious metal issues (eg the Arvernian fox type from Cornet (Nash 1978a, 157) and several Biturigan bronze and potin types (*ibid* 223)). Some bronze coinages are severely restricted in circulation, and are found predominantly on one site, which may therefore be regarded as their place of origin. Central sites which probably had bronze mints include Puy de Corent (Nash 1978a, 157), Gergovie (*ibid*, 125ff) and perhaps Châteaumeillant (*ibid*, 230). When coin finds from recent excavations at Levroux and Saint-Marcel in Indre have been analysed it is very likely that they will go far to identify the bronze issues local to those sites. Other coins are found widely scattered over Gaul, as a result of post-conquest circulation.

Bronze coinage was most widely issued and used in the decades after the Roman conquest, when the issue and use of precious metals largely ceased, partly because of Roman depredations, but mainly because the right to maintain an army, and therefore the very reason to issue a precious metal coinage, had been lifted by the fact of assimilation into the Roman empire (Nash 1978c). It was only after the conquest that bronze coins were hoarded, presumably because in the absence of precious metal coinages, they were for the first time called upon to act as a store of wealth as well as a medium of payment and exchange. There are therefore, of course, difficulties in deciding which bronze issues are certainly of pre-conquest origin, especially if specimens were not found at Alesia, but it is evident that in Central Gaul both before and after the Conquest the major settlements used—and many probably issued—bronze coinages. I would argue that all major settlements with sufficient resources, and certainly all with regional administrative functions, must have struck bronze coinages. The confinement of bronze coins to the larger centres of population and the fact that the majority of coin finds on most settlements are bronze, together with the absence of bronze hoards until after the conquest, suggests that bronze coinage had functions different from those of the precious metals, and I believe that they were issued to make day-to-day payments necessary for the running and upkeep of the towns themselves. Their confinement to such sites may largely be accounted for by their suitability for use in retail trade and subsistence markets such as would be found in all major towns. Bronze coin is also abundant on temple sites, partly no doubt as offerings (eg the ritual pits at Argentomagus/Saint-Marcel: *Gallia* (1974), 308); but also perhaps because in the countryside temples may have been the sites for periodic gatherings at which exchanges, some of which would involve the use of coin, took place.

First century coinages replace earlier Central Gaulish issues in several areas, from which it follows that the earlier issues must belong to a period before the settlement of the defended sites on which no earlier coins are found, ie the 2nd century BC in general. Clear examples of the replacement of earlier by later coinages are provided by the Aedui (Nash 1978a, 69–72), whose early gold coinage was replaced around the end of the 2nd century by a silver issue, itself replaced or accompanied by the mid 1st century with issues inscribed with the name of officials, including the historical Dumnorix. The territory of the Bituriges Cubi had both gold and silver issues in the 2nd century; the silver issues are found in the west of the area and are, almost without exception, found in hoards (Fig 5). Both this circumstance, which suggests non-recovery due to death or flight of their owners, and the worn condition of many of the dies which struck the coins themselves, suggests that the silver coinage of 2nd century Berry was issued in the course of serious military disturbances. The gold coins, on the other hand, are not found hoarded, but scattered around the iron-bearing areas of northern and central Berry where some of the few La Tène II graves known in Central Gaul have been recorded. Both silver and gold coins show a wide variety of types, which may be taken to indicate multiple authorship, in the light of documentary indications that before the 1st century BC political authority was widely spread among the Celtic nobility.

Areas where later coinages replaced earlier ones are particularly valuable as historical evidence; there were, however, many more, like the Arverni and Pictones, whose first coinages were late phase, 1st century, issues (Nash 1978, 201).

The principal contrasts between the early and late Central Gaulish coinages, therefore, are:

    1 The early coinages are exclusively of precious metal in high denominations: gold in units not less than the quarter-stater of 1.5g or more, and silver in units of over 3.0g.

    2 Earlier coins are never found on major defended settlements, and have in fact not yet been found in any well defined archaeological context.

    3 The number of different types in any area, each perhaps representing a very small issue, is higher in the 2nd than in the 1st century.

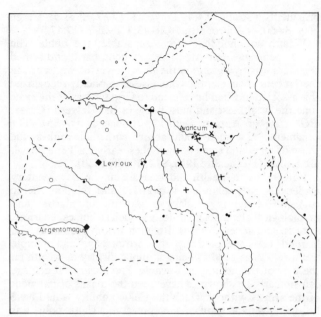

Fig 5 Berry in the 3rd and 2nd centuries BC: ○ ○ *2nd century silver hoard and stray find;* ● ● *3rd–2nd century gold hoard and stray find;* + *La Tène I burial;* × *La Tène II burial*

    4 The geographical distribution of the coinages immediately preceding the late phase is seldom well defined in Central Gaul because of the scarcity of specimens of any one type, with the exception of 2nd century silver in west Berry; the early Central Gaulish coinages are derived in type from the earliest gold coinage of Switzerland and the Rhineland, which itself had a very diffuse distribution, in stark contrast with the well defined 1st century gold distribution patterns (for early Helvetic staters, see Allen 1974; Nash 1978a, 84ff). In all cases early gold is of higher gold content than 1st century coins.

Explanation of changes in the use of coinage must rest on a prior understanding of the use of wealth by the Celts, since I believe that Celtic coinage must be regarded as a specialized form of wealth, subject to the same rules of use as other forms.

The Celtic aristocracy were warriors above all: this is how they appeared to their Mediterranean neighbours, and the social values which governed the allocation of resources in Celtic society were those of the aristocracy. Gold and silver ornaments, the means of feasting, horses, cattle, arms and, later, coinage, were the means of the traditional conduct of heroic life, and as such were in the control and gift of the aristocracy. Documentary evidence abounds to show that, at least in the eyes of the Greeks and Romans, the Celts were overwhelmingly preoccupied with wealth and warfare, and that the two were intimately connected. One of the earliest accounts of a Celtic population refers to the 4th century BC Celts recently arrived in northern Italy from across the Alps: 'Their possessions consisted of cattle and gold, because these were the only things they could carry around with them everywhere according to circumstances, and shift wherever they chose' (Polybius 2.17.11). Before the introduction of coinage, gold was possessed principally in the form of ornaments, which could be worn on the person, for instance as arm or neck rings; quite apart from archaeological finds of these items, classical literature contains many accounts of Gaulish warriors, of what in archaeological terms would be regarded as the Middle La Tène period, fighting naked or clothed, but always resplendent in gold ornaments (Strabo 4.4.5; Polybius 2.29.7, 2.31.5; Vergil *Aen.* 8.660, 662; Propertius 4.10.43; Caesar *BG* 7.47.5).

Wealth and nobility were inseparable; the noble who could spend most on gifts, feasts, a good bard, and armed retainers was by definition the most powerful, and even in the 1st century in Central Gaul Caesar implicitly recognized this association when he referred to Orgetorix as át the same time the wealthiest and most noble of the Helvetii (Caesar *BG* 1.2.1; cf Appian *Celt.* 12; Athenaeus iv. 36). The ornaments of women would accord with their rank as did those of men, and some of the richest early La Tène burials are female (Déchelette 1914, 914, 1088f, 1030).

References to wealth and treasure in the documentary evidence nearly all relate to warfare and religion. Celtic coinage frequently displays a mixture of martial and mythological elements in its design, such as horses, chariots, swords, and severed heads. Religion was in the hands of a learned class peopled by the aristocracy, and temple treasure was as good as being a public display of wealth on the part of the nobility as a whole. Precious metal coinage can similarly be shown to have been the means of payment of the armies without which the Celtic nobility would have lost its power and status. As the power of a Celtic noble was counted in terms of the number of his armed retainers (Polybius 2.17.12; Caesar *BG* 6.15.2), and as these would remain with him only so long as he maintained their support by his good performance in the field and in displays of hospitality at home, the use of wealth within the Celtic system of clientage is of great importance and is of direct relevance to the question of the introduction of coinage (Athenaeus iv. 36; Strabo 4.2.3; cf. Diodorus 5.26.2, Polybius 2.19.3–4, 11.3.1; Ammianus Marcellinus 15.12.4).

Wealth, then, was a prerequisite of social status among the Celts, and documentary sources provide an invaluable account of one of the ways in which control was exercised over the acquisition of wealth by those of inferior social position; it also illustrates one aspect of the relationship between the religious and warrior establishments.

Diodorus Siculus (5.27.3–4), drawing on the early 1st century account of Poseidonios, said of the Celts of southern Gaul that they would amass a great amount of gold which they turned into arm and neck ornaments and rings for both men and women. They also dedicated large amounts of gold to the gods in sacred precincts, and no native of the country would dare to touch it because of religious fear, even though the Celts were a covetous people. This fear of stealing dedicated treasure was not peculiar to the continental Celts. An example of what might happen to anyone who tampered with sacred treasure is related in striking fashion in an early Irish account in the voyage of Mael Dúin (Jackson 1971, 153–5). When the temple at Tolosa was sacked by the Romans in 106, an enormous amount of precious metal in the form of offerings was removed from it, 15 000 talents of unworked silver and gold according to Strabo (4.1.13). Caesar, too, commented on this practice of dedicating valuables to the gods (*BG* 6.17.3–5). He says that after battle, the spoils were generally dedicated and the animals sacrificed; no-one dared to touch the dedicated spoils. One may assume that, as in the case of the Romans themselves, a victorious warrior would in fact normally take a part of the spoils before dedication for distribution to his followers, but the rest was left for all to see, as a public monument to the prowess of the local nobility, in the sacred places. Caesar said that one could see heaps of them here and there; he certainly turned them to good use himself, for he returned immensely rich in gold from Gaul, mainly, as Suetonius records, stripped from temples (Suetonius *DJ* 54). It is hardly surprising, therefore, that excavations of temple sites invariably yield coins as well as remains of animals and ornaments.

Precious metal was used for making gifts and payments long before the use of coinage among the Celts. For instance, Polybius records that in 299 the Insubres and Boii of Cisalpine Gaul obtained the military assistance of kings Concolitanus and Aneroëstes of the Gaesatae over the Alps, with the intention of using them for a march against Rome, by pointing out that the Romans would provide rich spoil, and by giving them a lot of gold (Polybius 2.22.2, cf. 2.19.1, 2.34.2). Later, in a period when the use of coin was widespread in other parts of Gaul, the Arvernian king Louernios, in the mid 2nd century BC, is recorded by Poseidonios as scattering gold and silver to his followers in the course of a lavish display of hospitality lasting many days (Athenaeus iv. 49, 246c; Strabo 4.2.3). At this period the Arverni themselves had no coinage, and no coins of any other people datable to the 2nd century have been found on their territory. Louernios may, therefore, have been using valuables other than coin for his largesse. When the use of precious metal coin was well established, gold objects and ingots were often still hoarded with them.

The earliest uses of coin by the Celts were in those areas in which exchange of valuables already occurred. The earliest and most important was the use of gold coin for payment of services, and it was in service as mercenaries for Hellenistic overlords, especially the kings of Macedon, that the Celts learnt the use of coinage. The connection between the growth of centralized political power in Gaul which necessitated an increasing dependence on armed force, and the development of the use of coinage there from the 3rd century onwards must have been very close.

Colin Kraay argued (1964) that the payment of mercenaries was among the earliest uses of coin in Greece, and a similar point has been made by Keith Rutter (above, p 5). Griffith (1935) abundantly documented the role mercenary armies played in determining the expenditure of Greek governments. The example of the Transalpine Gaesatae, hired for their services by the northern Italian Celts in the 3rd century, and whose very name was thought to mean 'mercenaries', illustrates the freedom with which the Celts themselves would hire military assistance, in what was effectively an extension of their traditional system of maintaining armed retainers (Orosius 4.3.5). It is also clear, for instance from Polybius (2.26.5), that the mobility of certain high-value goods gave them special importance. It was important to mercenaries to be able to take home with them the wealth they had won. It is one clear advantage of gold or silver coin that it is both valuable and portable, and it is a characteristic of Celtic coinage in every area of Europe that the earliest denominations were very valuable.

It was therefore from the coin-using Mediterranean that the Celts first obtained coins, and so far as the Central Celts were concerned, it is likely, if only on the grounds of the systematic borrowing of early coin types from coinages of known mercenary employers, that the Celts encountered the use of coin in payments for their services as barbarian mercenaries. There is, however, substantial supporting evidence in documentary sources that the Celts were, during the late 4th and most of the 3rd centuries, the largest single barbarian component in the Macedonian armies of Philip II, Alexander III, and their successors, and that many cities around the Mediterranean, including Massilia and Carthage, similarly used Celtic mercenaries (Griffith 1935; Polybius 1.67.7; 3.41.9). Other cities using Celtic mercenaries may perhaps be deduced from the popularity of their coin types among some Celtic peoples, notably Emporiae and Rhode on the Catalan coast of Spain.

Barbarian mercenaries were paid in coin by their employers, whether or not there was any use for the coin in their countries of origin. Thus, for instance, the Balearic islanders, paid in silver by the Carthaginians, had to spend all their pay on wine and women before returning home because coin was not permitted there (Diodorus 5.17.4). During the period when they were most active as mercenaries, the Celts themselves did not strike coinage, and it is an open question what they actually did with their pay at home. In the Danubian region a certain amount of Macedonian coinage was hoarded from an early date (Preda 1973), but this was not the case in the western Celtic areas: perhaps a lot of it was converted into ornaments. But there is nonetheless valuable evidence in Greek sources for the rates of pay and magnitude of the sums spent on Celtic mercenaries by the Macedonians and Carthaginians; it was presumably the hard bargains the Celts struck and their behaviour on pay-day that earned them their widespread reputation for greed.

In the context of the mercenary rebellion in 241, Polybius mentions that the Carthaginians were forced to pay a gold stater each to their mercenaries for pressing expenses; more in fact was owed to them (Polybius 1.66–1.68). Livy (44.26) gives an account of the pay offered to the Bastarnae by king Perseus when he tried to hire them as mercenaries: 1 000 gold pieces for their king, 10 each for cavalrymen, and 5 each for infantry: this was probably the fee for the whole of their service, and gives some idea of the considerable value of a gold stater. Antigonus Gonatas hired some Gauls for an unknown period at the rate of one Macedonian stater per man; the whole army at the end of its service for him cost 30 talents (Griffith 1935, 293; Polyaenus 4.6.17).

The use of coinage for payments, therefore, was probably learnt in service for Hellenistic mercenary armies, and it is therefore wholly appropriate that when the Celts first began to strike their own coinages in the late 3rd and early 2nd centuries they used as models Macedonian and other Greek coins. Philip II, who was the first large-scale employer of Celtic mercenaries and whose coinage continued in use long after his death, provided the most commonly used model for Celtic coinage both in Gaul and in the Danubian basin.

The reasons for the introduction of coin in Celtic areas can only be guessed at. The first coinages were struck long before the settlement of sites which can be dated on archaeological grounds to the 1st century BC, and there are no archaeological contexts for the early phases of the coinage. The introduction of coinage is unlikely to have been a casual event in any area, and it seems at present probable that the earliest coinages in many Celtic areas— the Rhineland, Belgic Gaul, south-western Gaul and the Danube basin—commenced at around the same time. Those early issues most susceptible of dating on typological and metrological grounds may be placed between the course of the 3rd century and the early 2nd[4], and it is therefore apparent that reasons connected with the social and political development of the Celts must be sought to account for this phenomenon, in the same way in which the widespread settlement of defended sites late in the 2nd century and early in the 1st also requires a socio-political explanation. Unfortunately, in the absence of any documentary evidence for the history of the Gaulish Celts in the 3rd century, and in the almost total absence in Central Gaul of any archaeological trace of their settlement apart from coinage and a handful of warrior burials, it is difficult to say very much. The great migrations of the Celts across Europe came to an end during the 3rd century, and it is therefore likely that the later 3rd and 2nd centuries was a period during which a new pattern of territorial overlordship was imposed and consolidated in Gaul; the apparently disturbed conditions in western Berry suggested by the late 2nd century coin hoards deposited shortly before the settlement of the defended sites in the area are one legacy of this period.

I have argued elsewhere that the development of nucleated and defended settlements and the increase in luxury exchange with the Mediterranean during the late 2nd and 1st centuries must be seen as one outcome of the violent competition within the Celtic nobility for possession of territory, wealth, and armed retinues (Nash 1976; 1978a; forthcoming). I therefore offer the suggestion that the early coinages were instituted at a time when the now firmly rooted nobilities moved into a new phase of political and economic growth, which this time took the form not of migratory expansion but a combination of intensified exploitation of existing territory, and attempts on the part of individual noble groupings to control increasingly large areas. This is a hypothesis difficult to test with the meagre surviving evidence, but it would provide an appropriate context for the introduction of coinage as a convenient medium of payment for larger and more permanent armies necessary to provide the overt force needed to maintain such growth. The very fact of being able to issue a high-value coinage in significant quantities suggests that already in the late 3rd century there were some groups able to command exceptional resources. This is especially true of the Rhineland nobility, who issued one of the earliest gold coinages in Gaul.

Once the principle of striking coin for payments was accepted, its use for other purposes could follow, such as tribute, taxes, rents, bride-price, blood money, and fines; its use in exchange also became possible. As early as 219 BC Comontorius, and later Cavarus, leading the Celts inland of Byzantium, demanded successive payments of 3 000, 5 000, and 10 000 gold pieces and finally an annual tribute of 80 talents to secure their good behaviour (Polybius 4.46.3). This payment in coin was an alternative to payment in uncoined gold, which in the 4th century, for instance, the Celts had extorted from Rome, when Brennus obtained 1 000lb (Livy 5.48). By Caesar's time the use of coin was well established for payment of inducements or bribes (Caesar *BG* 7.63.2, 7.37.1, 1.9.3, 5.55.1, 6.6.1–2, 7.64.8). There were, however, some respects in which the introduction of coin undoubtedly permitted new developments, and the development of the late-phase coinages described above can be seen as one response to increasingly complex administrative and political needs.

The 1st century states in Central Gaul were different in important ways both from earlier Gaulish socio-political groupings of which records survive and from many of their neighbours in northern and western areas who preserved older social structures into the 1st century BC (Nash 1978b). Briefly, the characteristics of the 1st century *civitates* of Central Gaul were:

1 There was a strong central government, seemingly established in one leading defended settlement, which had sufficient authority over the constituent parts of the state to direct their political and military behaviour. This contrasts with the earlier and less centralized groupings, who, though they might acknowledge a common name and nationality, could not be coerced from the centre but had to be tackled noble by noble and fortress by fortress.

2 Although politically centralized in this sense, it is apparent that the 1st century *civitates* were nonetheless also federal. The major constituent parts or *pagi* seem to have had charge of their own military organization, and I have argued that they may sometimes have provided their own finances for their military contingents; there is every reason to think therefore that each *pagus* saw to its own taxes (see, for example, Caesar *BG* 1.18.3 for tax contracts).

3 The degree of centralization achieved by the 1st century Central *civitates* was such that their boundaries could be assumed almost unchanged by

the Roman administration, with the result that in Central Gaul alone it is possible with some confidence to reconstruct the autonomous *civitas* boundaries from those of the Roman period. Elsewhere in Gaul the Roman boundaries cut across and falsified earlier groupings, so that their territorial limits cannot be accurately recovered.

4 The government of the central *civitates* consisted of a narrowly constituted oligarchy, and there were publicly known laws which included strict rules to prevent, at least in theory, the usurpation of the entire power of the state by any single noble or his family. Membership of the Aeduan senate was restricted to one member of any family in any one generation; the chief magistracy was annual, and the magistrate could not leave the territory and thereby become a successful warrior while in charge of state resources. It is probable that these politically centralized states must in each case have undergone a period of deliberate reform, similar to that of Solon and Cleisthenes at Athens or Servius Tullius at Rome. The carefully constructed rules of government of these states are unlikely to have emerged haphazardly; provisions such as those for the composition of the Aeduan senate and election of the chief magistrate would have been unworkable without explicit definition of the status of the provinces or *pagi* of the state from which the nobility was drawn.

One of the acts of several early Mediterranean lawgivers was to regulate the weights and measures of their society. I suggest that the coinages of the 1st century BC, with their idiosyncratic weights and finenesses, as well as their self-conscious types, may be one legacy of an episode of political and administrative changes in the course of formation of the 1st century *civitas*.

The modifications in political structure and the very marked change in settlement pattern in the late 2nd and early 1st centuries, which was most obviously expressed in the growth of large nucleated settlements, must have occasioned the need for increasingly regular payments on the part of the authorities. It is one of the marked features of the late-phase coinages that they are both much more abundant than their predecessors in their output and also much baser in precious metal content. Most of Central Gaul is without very large sources of precious metal ores, so that any very heavy requirements for payment, particularly in gold, would of necessity require a debasement of the currency to spin out available resources, given that stocks of precious metal stored in temples appears to have been inviolable. The expenses of the Caesarian war caused the most marked debasement, and in western areas with Armorican types of stater, the precious metal content of the coins dropped virtually to zero (Nash 1978a, 246). But even before the war the metal content of all gold coinages was low enough to suggest that state resources were strained; it is not therefore surprising that when the need for an abundant small value coinage was experienced, most towns turned to bronze rather than silver.

The sharp change in coin types generally which marks the beginning of the late-phase coinages, and the introduction of bronze coinage for the first time, is not a socially and politically neutral occurrence. Fresh types peculiar to each *civitas* or part of a *civitas* suggest a new degree of political selfconsciousness; early Central Gaulish gold coinages, in particular, differed little in overall type from one another, and it is the minor symbols and overall style which normally differentiate them, rather than the composition of the types as a whole. The lighter and baser 1st century coinages were better suited than their predecessors to the increased needs for government payments which accompanied political centralization and the administration of internal taxes and fines on a larger scale than before. The introduction of bronze coinage at some point after the changes in the precious metals is likely to have occurred to facilitate the administration of towns and perhaps especially to provide subsistence money for persons permanently employed on official tasks, for instance military duty, and who had no means of subsistence from the countryside. Coin paid to such persons would, as in Mediterranean towns and cities, have been spent in retail markets for food and small items, in the towns themselves or at periodic markets, and it is significant that the full development of Gaulish bronze currency did not occur until after the Roman conquest, in a period of rapid growth in the settlement of towns in Central Gaul.

Notes

1 Some *civitates*—for instance the Aedui, Bituriges, and the authors of the silver severed head group—seem to have struck silver on the 'standard' quinarius weight of 1.80–1.90g. Others, notably the Pictones and Arverni, struck silver on their own metrological standards (Nash 1978a, 138ff, 250ff). This partly accounts for the fact that 'standard' coins are diffused widely, especially after the conquest, while Arvernian and Pictonian silver tends to be restricted to home territories. Even in the 2nd century, coinages of different types differed somewhat in weight and fineness (eg coins in the Tayac hoard: Kellner 1970), but the differences were more pronounced in the 1st century. This has led some authors (eg Colbert de Beaulieu 1973, 183–92, 234) to suggest economic chaos and weakness on the part of the issuing authorities and confinement of types to home territory on account of their unacceptability abroad. This is a necessary inference only if it is assumed that coins were made for the purpose of export in trade (*ibid*, 172). If, however, they were issued instead as a means of making official payments, it follows that a large proportion of the coinage would normally stay within the area of influence of the issuing authority in a continuous cycle of payments going out and taxes and fines coming in.
2 Nash 1978a, 246ff, 250ff. Arvernian silver is not hoarded with gold either, so that identification of mint is based on type and distribution alone. Arvernian silver appears to be a fraction of the gold series and was perhaps not regarded as a particularly suitable form of wealth storage where gold was available, while in Poitou gold and silver were equally hoarded, but largely separately, as though issued and used separately.
3 The Lemovices are a problem. Two coinages may have been issued within their territory: the base gold crane and trefoil series (Nash 1978a, 280ff), and silver with severed head (*ibid*, 285ff). But neither coinage has a sufficiently clear distribution pattern for its origin to be confidently established, while the prehistory of the Lemovices is less well documented than that, for instance, of the Bituriges. It is therefore an open question whether these two coinages were Lemovican (thus comparable with the Biturigan or Pictonian coinages) or of other origin.
4 Third century BC dates for early coinage: Allen 1974 (Rhineland), Scheers 1978 (Belgic Gaul), Preda 1973 (Danubian basin), Nash 1978a (Central Gaul). Against these, Dr Karel Castelin proposes a date well into the 2nd century for the first coinages (1978), and Dr Colbert de Beaulieu holds a late chronology especially for second-phase issues (1973; cf Nash 1975).

Bibliography

Allen, D F, 1974 The philippus in Switzerland and the Rhineland, *Rev suisse numis*, 42–74
Blanchet, A, 1905 *Traité des monnaies gauloises*
Büchsenschütz, O, & Ralston, I, 1975 Découverte d'un *murus gallicus* à Levroux (Indre), *Gallia*, 27–48
Castelin, K, 1978 Wann begann die keltische Goldprägung?, *Money Trend*, **10**, 10
Colbert de Beaulieu, J-B, 1955 Numismatique celtique d'Alésia, *Rev Belge Numis*, **101**, 55–83
Colbert de Beaulieu, J-B, 1971 La trouvaille de monnaies gauloises de Saint-Pierre-de-Maille, *Gallia*, 3–16
Colbert de Beaulieu, 1973 *Traité de numismatique celtique*, **I**
Cothenet, A, 1968 Les monnaies gauloises d'Argentomagus, *RAC*, 204–11
Déchelette, J, 1914 *Manuel d'archéologie préhistorique, celtique et gallo-romaine* **II.3**
Griffith, G T, 1935 *The mercenaries of the Hellenistic world*
Jackson, K H, 1971 *A Celtic miscellany*

Kellner, H–J, 1970 Der Fund von Tayac, ein Zeugnis des Cimbernzuges?, *JNG*, 13–47

Kraay, C M, 1964 Hoards, small change, and the origin of coinage, *J Hellenic Stud*, **84**, 76–91

Nash, D, 1975 The chronology of Celtic coinage in Gaul: the Arvernian 'hegemony' reconsidered, *Numis Chron*, **15**, 7e ser, 204–18

Nash, D, 1976 The growth of urban society in France, in Cunliffe B W, & Rowley R T (eds), *Oppida: the beginnings of urbanisation in barbarian Europe*, 95–133

Nash, D, 1978a *Settlement and coinage in Central Gaul c 200–50 BC*

Nash, D, 1978b Territory and state formation in Central Gaul, in Green D, Haselgrove C, & Spriggs S (eds), *Social organisation and settlement: contributions from anthropology, archaeology and geography*, 455–75

Nash, D, 1978c Plus ça change . . . : currency in Central Gaul from Julius Caesar to Nero, in Carson R A G, & Kraay C M (eds) *Scripta Nummaria Romana: essays presented to Humphrey Sutherland*, 12–31

Nash, D, forthcoming *Celtic society in western Europe, c600–500 BC*

Preda, C, 1973 *Monedele Geto-Dacilor*

Scheers, S, 1978 *Traité de numismatique celtique* **II:** *La Gaule Belgique*

The beginning of coinage in Belgic Gaul

This paper deals with two important aspects of the coinage in Belgic Gaul: the origins of the coinage and its evolution after the Gallic war.

If it is true that the coins of Belgic Gaul developed, at some moment in their history, characteristics inherent at the very region where they were struck, it is wrong to think that the origin of coinage in this part of Gaul has no relation with the beginning of coinage in Gallia Comata.

Coinage in Belgic Gaul started in the region of Amiens with imitations of the staters of Tarentum, struck at the end of the 4th and the beginning of the 3rd century BC[1] (Fig 6, 1–11). The fact that, from the beginning, the influence of the stater of Philip II of Macedon is noticeable in the pseudo-legend of the coins with bearded head implies either the existence in other parts of Gaul of Philip II staters or, more probably, of imitations of these coins.

It is striking that in the five cases where Gaulish gold coins imitate Greek coins, the Greek prototypes clearly belong to the same period, namely the end of the 4th and the first half of the 3rd century BC: the staters of Philip II of Macedon were struck chiefly by his son Alexander the Great (336–23 BC) and his successors, Philip III Arrhidaios (323–16 BC) and Cassander (316–297 BC).[2] The stater of Lysimachos, with the Ammon-horned head, imitated by a series of gold staters and quarter staters from Eastern Gaul (de la Tour 1892, pl XVI, nos 3518, 3522) (Fig 6, 12), was struck between 323 and 281 BC (but posthumous issues went on until the 1st century BC).[3] A rare half-stater, struck in the 2nd century BC in Normandy (Scheers 1975, pl XVI, 268), imitates on the reverse the lion of the coins of Miletus, struck between 350 and 190 BC (Head 1963, 585–6) (Fig 6, 13–14), while a stater found at Nancy (Muret & Chabouillet 1889, nos 3652–3; Blanchet 1905, 217, fig 56), imitates on the obverse the head of Parthenope on the didrachms struck at Neapolis between 300 and 240 BC (Sambon 1903, 232–41; Brunetti 1955, 5–34) (Fig 6, 15–16). It is also significant that the gold stater of Cyrenaica, found on the beach of Lampaul-Ploudalmézeau (France, Finistère) was struck between 322 and 313 BC.[4]

Greek coins of different origins minted at the end of the 4th and the beginning of the 3rd century BC, evidently entered the Gallic world at some time in the 3rd or 2nd century BC, but can we state at precisely what moment this penetration occurred? This question is important because it is connected intimately with that of the genesis of the first Gaulish coins. Since there is no written record directly applicable to these important events in Gaulish economic life, we must look for other evidence.

Recently, Dr K Castelin of Prague presented a scheme for the evolution of Gaulish coins based on reduction of weight. He stated that the first imitations of Philip II of Macedon in Gaul were probably struck around 150 BC[5] (Fig 7). The first staters of the Ambiani, the Gallo-Belgic A staters, he argued were struck only after the invasions of the Cimbri, ie after 100 BC. The half-staters of the Ambiani, bearing the head of Hera and the Dioscuri, which show a high weight and a pure alloy, could have been struck at approximately 130 BC or even somewhat later, perhaps 110 BC, since a half-stater of 4.16g corresponds to a stater of 8.32g. The unique quarter-stater, having the weight of 2.07g, however, corresponds to a stater of 8.68g, which would place the beginning of this coinage at about 150 BC. From this new chronological classification, based primarily on a gradual and regular fall of the weight of Gaulish gold coins, we must conclude that the Gaulish tribes started their imitations approximately 150–100 years after the minting of the Greek prototypes. Is such a theory acceptable?

Let us consider the period in which the Greek coins were introduced into Gaul. Since previous investigations were concerned mainly with the introduction into Gaul of the staters of Philip II of Macedon, we are obliged to take them also into account.

There is scarcely any agreement about when the philippus was introduced into Gaul. Brooke placed this event in the 2nd century BC, on account of the fact that the philippus first appeared in Rome in the early 2nd century BC (Brooke 1933, 88–98). He considered Rome as the only purveyor to Gaul of the philippi. But the occurrence in south Germany and north Switzerland of imitations of the stater with corn-ear struck at Amphipolis, with heavy weight (8.29g) and rich alloy (92–90% Au) seems to point to the Danube as another possible way by which the philippi reached the Western Celts. In fact, although the Eastern Celts preferred to imitate the silver tetradrachms of Philip II, the philippus staters were frequently hoarded in Romania and Bulgaria at the end of the 4th and in the 3rd centuries BC.[6] It seems only natural that some of them reached Gaul by way of the Danube. On the other hand, of the six genuine staters of Philip II of Macedon discovered in Gaul, three have been found in coastal regions: Pons (Charente-Maritime), Landerrouat (Gironde), and Avène (Hérault).[7] This seems to point to their arrival by sea rather than by overland route along the Rhône and Saône as Brooke supposed. The supply of philippi to Gaul seems, therefore not to have relied entirely upon Rome.

Dr J-B Colbert de Beaulieu emphasizes (1973, 198–200) that there were a variety of ways for the Gauls to acquire Greek coins. For example, Gauls frequently acted as mercenaries in the Mediterranean World,[8] but trade with Massalia could also have obtained gold coins for the Gauls. Indeed, ancient writers testify that gold was used in Massalia.[9] The greatest part of gold coins circulating in the Mediterranean world was certainly composed of staters of Philip II of Macedon. The hoard found at Tarentum in 1883 and buried in the 3rd century BC contained 80 staters of Philip II of Macedon, 5 of Alexander III, and only 7 staters of Tarentum (Thompson *et al* 1973, no 1932). We must also realize that ships from Carthage and, probably, from other Greek cities such as Massalia circumnavigated the coasts of Gaul (as shown by the voyage of Pytheas in the 4th century BC). They will have disembarked here and there in search of commercial advantages, if not for more pressing purposes such as repairs. It seems only to be expected that on meeting with the inhabitants of the country, goods would be exchanged for coins. We might note that the stater of Cyrenaica, found on the beach of Finistère, has been linked to the voyage of Pytheas.

In view of these early contacts with the Mediterranean world, we can accept that Greek coins had already reached Gaul in the 3rd century BC. But this does not mean that imitation started immediately. In fact, as long as the import of Greek originals satisfied the needs of the native population, imitation was not needed. Thus, the intro-

Fig 6 Greek prototypes and their Gaulish copies: for details see note 1. 1 Berlin, coll Imhoof-Blümer; 2 London, British Museum (Tarentine coin); 3 BN 10195; 4 BN Greek coin (Tarentine coin); 5 BN 10203; 6 London, British Museum (Tarentine coin); 7 Péronne 278; 8 Péronne 279; 9 Stüttgart, Württembergisches Landesmuseum; 10 BN Greek coin 770 (Tarentine coin); 11 BN Greek coin 281 (Tarentine coin); 12 New York, American Numismatic Society; 13 Péronne 268; 14 Paris, BN 1737 (Coin of Miletus); 15 BN 3652; 16 Bruxelles, Cabinet des Médailles (Coin of Neapolis) (BN = Muret & Chabouillet 1889)

duction of Greek staters to Gaul provides a *terminus post quem* for the imitations, but not an absolute date for their beginning.

In his newly developed theory (Fig 7), Castelin provides a chronological scheme by making use of the gradual reduction of the weight of the gold coins. He thus traces the chronology of these coins from the most recent ones to the oldest ones. This theory is based on two assumptions. The first, derived from Colbert de Beaulieu (1973, 213), states that, after the fall of the Arverni in 121, there arose a profusion of gold coins having a weight between 7.95g and 7.80g. The second assumption is drawn from a joint publication by J-Cl Richard and Dr Colbert de Beaulieu (1969, 92) and declares that most of the cities in Gaul acquired the right of minting between 100 and 80 BC. According to this theory, the fall of the Arvernian empire, followed by the invasion of the Cimbri, is considered as the turning-point in the monetary history of Gaul. But in the absence of both archaeological evidence and of hoards of the earlier period, it is difficult to verify the opinion expressed by Dr Castelin.

While Dr Castelin proposes a late start for the native coinage in Gaul, he does not comment upon the fact that the prototypes are not contemporary but are coins struck at the end of the 4th and in the first half of the 3rd centuries BC.

It is difficult to understand how the coins of Tarentum and Neapolis reached Gaul, if it was not shortly after they were struck. It must be remembered that these coins, especially those of Tarentum, were struck during a limited period and in comparatively small quantities, and that their area of circulation was usually restricted. We must conclude therefore that Dr Castelin omits to consider certain vital factors directly relevant to the problem. We might also question if the fall in the weights has been as regular and as rapid as Dr Castelin supposes.

If Castelin's theory were to be confirmed, it would bring down the date of the first coinage in Belgic Gaul to approximately 130 BC. I preferred to date the first gold coins of the Ambiani (ie the half-staters) to the last half of the 3rd and the first half of the 2nd centuries BC on the assumption of direct contacts by sea between Tarentum and the Ambiani. The repeated imitation of coins from Tarentum excludes the supposition that the choice of the different prototypes happened only by accident. It is true that these imitations are not always evident, because the Celtic stylization greatly altered the Greek representation, but in all the cases where Tarentine influence has been shown, the resemblance between the Gaulish and the Tarentine coins is striking. It is, for instance, very clear for the horseman with shield on

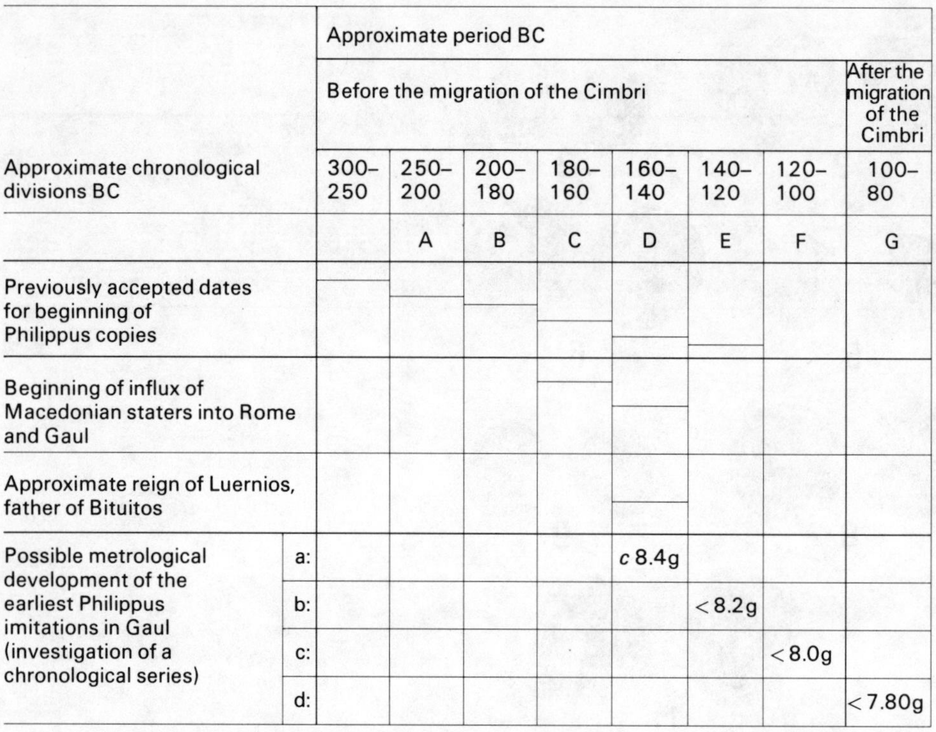

	Approximate period BC							
	Before the migration of the Cimbri							After the migration of the Cimbri
Approximate chronological divisions BC	300–250	250–200	200–180	180–160	160–140	140–120	120–100	100–80
		A	B	C	D	E	F	G
Previously accepted dates for beginning of Philippus copies								
Beginning of influx of Macedonian staters into Rome and Gaul								
Approximate reign of Luernios, father of Bituitos								
Possible metrological development of the earliest Philippus imitations in Gaul (investigation of a chronological series) — a:						*c* 8.4g		
b:							< 8.2g	
c:								< 8.0g
d:								< 7.80g

Fig 7 The beginnings of Celtic coinage in Gaul (after Castelin 1978)

the quarter-staters of series I and for the bearded head on the half-staters of series II. If the new chronology of Dr Castelin is confirmed, it would not dispose of our theory about direct contact by sea between Tarentum and the Ambiani: it would mean only that the Ambiani waited a little longer before substituting their own coins for Greek prototypes.

The preceding discussions make it clear that the date ascribed to the beginning of coinage in Gaul is still a subjective one. In any case, there must have been, at some moment in the 3rd or the 2nd centuries BC, a stimulus strong enough to encourage several tribes in Gallia Comata quite simultaneously to inaugurate their own coinage. It is no longer justifiable to give the Arverni the sole responsibility for these different coinages. There is no longer any doubt that at least seven independent centres struck the first great series of imitations of the philippi[10] (Fig 8, 17–23). In Belgic Gaul, the Ambiani initiated coinage a little later than the tribes of Gallia Comata: this much is demonstrated by the lower weight of their earliest coins and the imitation on them of the name of Philippus.

Coinage in Belgic Gaul after the Gallic war

The Gallic war completely disturbed the monetary policy of the Belgic tribes. At the end of the war, the gold coinages had disappeared and were superseded by series in silver and bronze. No direct testimony describes this change, but the currency gives ample proof of it. The 449 coins lost in 52 at Alesia were, with ten exceptions, silver and bronze coins (246 silver, 140 bronze coins, and 53 potin coins) (Colbert de Beaulieu 1955a, 55–83). Post-war settlements contain mostly only silver and bronze coins. Some hoards buried shortly after the end of the war (eg Vernon, buried in 45 BC: Scheers 1977a, 901–2, hoard 90) contain scarcely any gold coins.

The great variety of silver and, in Belgic Gaul especially, of bronze coins is explained in terms of the breaking up of the *civitas* in favour of the pagi. This evolution had started

already during the war, when the Meldi broke away from the Suessiones in 57 BC and obtained, together with their independence, the right of minting (Colbert de Beaulieu & Desbordes 1964, 101; Scheers 1977a, 73–4). But this political evolution increases the discomfiture of the numismatist since there is little known about the pagi in the second half of the 1st century BC. Caesar pays, indeed, little attention to these divisions of the *civitas*. The study of the post-war coinages is seriously hampered by our ignorance of the political reality, and it is only by using the names of the Caesarian tribes that these coinages can be approximately localized.

Our inability to analyse the situation is clearly demonstrated by the Treviri. The mint on the opidum of the Titelberg produced, in all probability, seven different series: the bronze coins of Arda (Fig 8, 24–8), Hirtius and Carrinas (Fig 8, 29–30), the later silver coins with a sitting personage (Fig 8, 31), and three series of cast coins: with boar (Fig 8, 32), with facing animals (Fig 8, 33), and with horse (Fig 8, 34).[11] Nearly all those coins were minted before 30 BC (specimens have been found in an archaeological layer dating to before 30 BC). The only exceptions are the scarce bronze coins of Carrinas, which can otherwise be dated by reference to the career of Carrinas who became proconsul of Gallia in 30 BC, and the cast coins with facing animals which cannot be dated at all. It is clear that all these coinages, minted between 50 and 30 BC, cannot have served to meet only the needs of the population of the Titelberg. We can with some probability ascribe to a *pagus*, or to a small independent tribe occupying part of the Treviran territory, the silver coins with the sitting personage. They were first struck in the neighbourhood of the Marberg and were already circulated before 52 BC. The reason why the mint was transferred to the Titelberg cannot be ascertained. There is no doubt that the coinage of Arda belongs to the population living on the Titelberg. The coins of this chief are the commonest ones on the *oppidum*, constituting 38.73% of all the Gaulish coins found on this site. But it remains uncertain what was the relation between

Fig 8 Gaulish imitations of philippi (17–23), and coins minted at the Titelberg (24–34); for details see p 20. 17 BN 3614; 18 Bésançon, Bibliothèque Municiple 41; 19 BN 4542; 20 BN 3432; 21 Saint-Germain-en-Laye, Musée des Antiquités Nationales 2448; 22 Bourges, Musée 959.29.1; 23 BN 4832; 24 BN 8841; 25 Luxembourg, Musée de l'Etat A 41; 26 BN 8849; 27 Luxembourg, Musée de l'Etat 224; 28 BN 8853; 29 BN 9243; 30 Stuttgart, Württembergisches Landesmuseum SU. 526; 31 München, Staatliche Münzsammlung; 32 BN 8445; 33 Cologne, Römisch-Germanisches Museum B 10761; 34 BN 8133 (BN = Muret & Chabouillet 1889)

the coinage of Arda, which may have started after the Treviran revolt in 51 BC, and the coins of Hirtius, minted from 45 BC onwards. The same is true for the three series of cast coins.

When we compare the weights of Arda's bronze coins and Hirtius's coins, we see that the weights of the most recent coins of Arda are appreciably lighter than 2.00g, while the coins of Hirtius weigh between 4.00g and 2.00g. The problem is to know if, supposing that the two coinages are struck for the same people, the two series are in part contemporaneous or if the coins of Hirtius succeed those of Arda. In the latter case, it is possible that Hirtius's coins replaced completely those of Arda in 45 BC as a Roman-inspired coinage, which would explain their higher weight. It would be unprecedented if, of two successive coinages, the more recent should have higher weights than the older one if we did not see that the coins of Carrinas were on Hirtius's weight-standard. In spite of their lesser value, such a phenomenon would seem exceptional even for bronze coins.

In this case the study of the find-spots, so relevant in other examples, does not permit us to make a suitable attribution, because their distribution shows no specific concentration in any part of the Treviran territory.

The same confused situation appears in the large number of coinages ascribed to the Suessiones: five bronze series and two, or perhaps three, series of cast coins. The excavations conducted by J Debord on the fortified site of Villeneuve-Saint-Germain have shed an interesting light on some cast coinages attributed to the Suessiones. The site lies east of Soissons and 6km from the famous *oppidum* of Pommiers, considered to be Noviodunum, the principal *oppidum* of the Suessiones. The excavations, conducted from 1973 to 1978, yielded 108 coins and one fragment. Several tribes are represented, but the most frequent coins, as might be expected, are those of the Suessiones. Yet the composition of this collection is totally different from that found at Pommiers. The coins of the Suessiones found at Pommiers were mostly bronze coins inscribed CRICIRV (956 examples) (Fig 9, 35) together with issues in gold and silver, and coins with the janiform head (349 examples)[12] and only a few cast coins (17 examples in total). At Villeneuve-Saint-Germain the situation is totally different. The coins of CRICIRV are absent and only four coins with janiform head of class II (Fig 9, 36), showing an ornate obverse and a rigid lion on the reverse, have been found. On the other hand, the cast coins are in the majority: 65 specimens of four varieties, ie 60% of all the Gaulish coins

Fig 9 Coins of the Suessiones: for details see note 13. 35 Saint-Germain-en-Laye, Musée des Antiquités Nationales 3437; 36–40 Villeneuve-Saint-Germain, recent excavations

found on this site. From the three types with horse[13] on the reverse (Fig 9, 37–9), formerly given to the Silvanectes, and considered by us as three different classes of the same Suessiones coinage, five specimens have been found of class I (BN 7862) (Fig 9, 37), 40 of class II (BN 7870) (Fig 9, 38), and only one of class III (BN 7859) (Fig 9, 39), while the series with floral ornament[14] (Fig 9, 40) was present with 19 specimens. The most frequent coins at Villeneuve-Saint-Germain are thus the coins with horse of class II, which represent 37% of all Gaulish coins found at the site, and the coins with floral ornament, which represent 17.5%. The frequency with which the coins with horse of class II occur at Villeneuve-Saint-Germain implies that they constituted the local coinage of the place. The same observation can perhaps be applied to the coins with floral ornament. These figures therefore suggest that a mint was located at Villeneuve-Saint-Germain. This supposition is confirmed by the occurrence of moulds, such as have been found elsewhere in and outside France (eg on Mont Beuvray and at the Titelberg) which demonstrates the presence of metalworking on the site. It should be pointed out that from the three different types with horse, attributed to the Suessiones, only one seems to have been local to Villeneuve-Saint-Germain and had probably been struck there. This could mean either that the two other types are posterior to the occupation of the site or that they were struck elsewhere. One ought probably to ascribe a different origin to these coins, in spite of the affinity of their types. The weights seem to corroborate our opinion, but only where the coins of class I are concerned. These are slightly heavier than those of class II and range from 5.79g to 4.20g. The weights of the coins with horse of class II are more spread, but the majority of the coins weigh between 4.99g and 3.00g. The coins with floral ornament have the same weight-curve. Of the coins with horse of class III, only four weights are known, too few for firm judgment.

We must emphasize the great difference between Pommiers and Villeneuve-Saint-Germain. Of the two series struck at Pommiers, those with CRICIRV and those with janiform head, only the coin with janiform head is present and only in a late version and in a very small quantity. This seems to indicate that the occupation of Villeneuve-Germain was more recent than that of Pommiers. The vicinity of the two cities, indeed, makes it impossible that

there would not have been any contact between them. Pommiers is considered to have been extensively occupied during the Gallic war (Colbert de Beaulieu 1955b). In fact, the coinage of CRICIRV is struck during the war. Afterwards, the site was not completely abandoned, as the finds of Gaulish and Roman coins show, but seems to have been occupied at intervals or only by a few people. The theory may therefore been formulated that the population of Pommiers moved to Villeneuve-Saint-Germain shortly after the war. In this case, the people did not continue their original coinage, but broke completely with their tradition and created instead two series of cast coins, one with horse and one with floral ornament. It is not possible to ascribe the two other series with horse to a particular site. We must wait patiently for excavations to throw light on this puzzle.

Notes

1 Scheers 1977a, 27–37, 219–28, pl I, 1–26. The half-staters bearing the head of Hera on the obverse and the Dioscuri on the reverse (*ibid*, pl I, 1–2) are imitations of similar staters struck at Tarentum in 315 (Ravel 1947, 4, nos 21–2), or, as has recently been suggested, in 302 (Robinson 1971, 30). The horseman on the quarter-stater with a Hera head on the obverse (Scheers 1977a, pl I, 4) is copied from a Tarentine stater struck between 342 and 333 (Robinson 1971, 28–9, no 31). The half-staters and quarter-staters with a bearded head on the obverse and a biga on the reverse imitate on the obverse the bearded head of Zeus which appears on the staters struck by Alexander I, king of Epirus, in 322 or on a similar stater struck by Pyrrhus in 320 and 272 BC (Robinson 1971, 30–1, nos 40–1). The biga on the reverse imitates the biga on the stater struck by Alexander I, king of Epirus, in 334 (Ravel 1947, 3, no 16; Robinson 1971, 29, no 34) and by Pyrrhus about 261 BC (Ravel 1947, 5–6, no 28): the long hair of the driver is a misinterpretation of the flying cloak of the driver on the Tarentine prototypes.

2 Le Rider 1977, 433–4 and 442. The first issues are struck about 345 or 342, but the minting only becomes important from 340/336 on, ie in the last years of Philippus or after his death and during the reign of Alexander. The minting ceased in Amphipolis in 315 and in Pella in 310 BC, but there may have been some rare issues between 310 and 294.

3 From 88 to 85 BC, Mithridates (120–64 BC) struck coins of the types of Lysimachus in the mints on the Black Sea (Thompson 1968, 183–200, pl 23–5).

4 Colbert de Beaulieu & Giot 1961, 324–31. The coin is a stater with the name of the magistrate Polianthes, struck between 322 and 313 (Naville 1951, 45–6, pl IV, 90–5).

5 Castelin 1978a, 9–11; 1978b, 8–11; 1978c, 10–12. This paper gives the latest evolution of the ideas of Dr Castelin: the coinage in Gaul started in the period between 160 and 140 BC, whereas in his earlier papers this event is placed between 180 and 160 BC.

6 Thompson *et al* 1973, nos 395, 399, 408, 427, 727, 728, 775, 777, 796, 797, 809, 810, 853, 958.

7 The three other finds are: Buzançais (Indre), Méry-sur-Cher (Cher), and Saint-Sylvain-Montaigut (Creuse). Another stater of Philip II was found at Milton, near Sittingbourne (Kent).

8 The Carthaginians frequently employed Gallic mercenaries. First mentioned in the war against Timoleon of Syracuse in 342/1 (Diodorus, XVI, 73, 3, but Plutarch, *Timoleon* 28, 6, does not mention them), Gallic mercenaries served in the two Carthaginian wars against Rome (Frontinus, *Stratagemata* III, 16, 2–3; Diodorus, XXIII, 8, 3; Polybius, I, 43, 4 (first war) and Polybius, VIII, 30, 1, 4, 9 (second war)). At Marseille, Gallic mercenaries are testified in 218 BC (Livy, XXI, 26, 5; Polybius, III, 41, 9).

9 Strabo, IV, 1, 5: the dowry amounted to 100 gold staters, plus 5 for clothing and 5 for jewelry. Theophrastus mentions that the carbuncles found at Carthage and in the neighbourhood of Marseille were sold at 40 staters a piece (Theophrastus, *De lapidibus* III, 18).

10 In the beginning there were seven main series:

    1 the series which imitates the symbols of the mint of Abydos: AP, thunderbolt, and corn ear, is localized in east France (Fig 8, 17);

    2 the series which imitates the Ammon-horned head of the stater of Lysimachus is localized in the French departments of Jura and Doubs (Fig 8, 18);

    3 the series which imitates, in Central Gaul, the symbols of the mint of Lampsacus, AP and a bust (Fig 8, 19);

    4 near the mouth of the Garonne is localized the series with the trident, symbol of the mints of Pella and Amphipolis (Fig 8, 20);

    5–6 two series which bear the *cantharos* of the mint of Pella are too widespread to be localized (Fig 8, 21–22);

    7 the series which shows the corn ear of the mint of Amphipolis is localized in south Germany and north Switzerland (Fig 8, 23).

11 Arda: de la Tour 1892, XXVI, 8839, 8849, 8852; Scheers 1977b, pl II, 26–32; Scheers 1977a, 150, pl IX, 239–53.
Hirtius: de la Tour 1892, XXXVII, 9235; Scheers 1977a, 152, 665–8, pl XX, 564–6; Scheers 1977b, pl II, 36–7.
sitting figure: de la Tour 1892, XXXVIII, 9383; Scheers 1977a, 117–18, 500–3, pl XIII, 342–3; Scheers 1977b, pl II, 46.
boar: de la Tour 1892, XXXIII, 8445; Scheers 1977a, 174, 782–4, pl XXV, 698–9; Scheers 1977b, pl II, 39.
facing animals: de la Tour 1892, XXX, 7465; Scheers 1977a, 174–6, 784–7, pl XXV, 700–2; Scheers 1977b, pl II, 40–1.
horse: de la Tour 1892, XXXII, 8133; Scheers 1977a, 176, 787–8, pl XXV, 703–4; Scheers 1977b, pl II, 44.

12 Criciru de la Tour 1892, XXXII, 7951; Scheers 1977a, 143–4, 377–8, pl VII, 191–3.
janiform: de la Tour 1892, XXXII, 8106; Scheers 1977a, 144, 650–4, pl XIX, 544–7.

13 de la Tour 1892, XXXI, 7859, 7862, 7870; Scheers 1977a, 173, 772–6, pl XXIV, 691–3.

14 de la Tour 1892, XXXI, 7873; Scheers 1977a, 776–8, pl XXIV, 694.

Bibliography

Blanchet, A, 1905 *Traité des monnaies gauloises*

Brooke, GC, 1933 The Philippus in the west and the Belgic invasions of Britain, *Numis Chron*

Brunetti, L, 1955 Contributo alla cronologia delle zecche di Velia e Neapolis, *Riv ital numis*, 57, 5–34

Castelin, K, 1978a Gewicht und Zeit in der gallischen Goldmünzung, *Money Trend*, 10,1, 9–11

Castelin, K, 1978b Die schönen Ambiani-Statere mit 'breitem Schrötling', *ibid*, 10,3, 8–11

Castelin, K, 1978c Wann began die keltische Goldprägung in Gallien?, *ibid*, 10,11, 10–12

Colbert de Beaulieu, J-B, 1955a Numismatique celtique d'Alésia, *Rev Belge Numis*, 101, 55–83

Colbert de Beaulieu, J-B, 1955b Peut-on dater par la numismatique l'occupation d'un oppidum?, *Revue archéologique de l'Est*, 6, 260–70

Colbert de Beaulieu, J-B, 1973 *Traité de numismatique celtique* 1: *Méthodologie des ensembles*

Colbert de Beaulieu, J-B, & Desbordes, J-M, 1964 'Criciru' et 'Roveca', les Belges sur la Marne, *Rev belge numis*, 110, 101

Colbert de Beaulieu, J-B, & Giot, P-R, 1961 Un statère d'or de Cyrénaïque découvert sur une plage bretonne et la route atlantique de l'étain, *Bull Soc préhist franc*, 58, 324–31

de la Tour, H, 1892 *Atlas de monnaies gauloises*

Head, B V, 1963 *Historia Numorum* (reprint of 1911 edn)

Le Rider, C, 1977 *Le monnayage d'argent et d'or de Philippe II frappé en Macédoine de 359 à 294*

Muret, E & Chabouillet, A, 1889 *Catalogue des monnaies gauloises de la Bibliothèque nationale*

Naville, L, 1951 *Les monnaies d'or de la Cyrénaïque de 450 à 250 av J-C*

Ravel, O E, 1947 *Descriptive catalogue of the collection of Tarentine coins formed by M P Vlasto*

Richard, J-Cl, & Colbert de Beaulieu, J-B, 1969 La numismatique de la Gaule et la numismatique de la Narbonnaise, *Revue d'études ligures*, 35, 92

Robinson, E S G, 1971 *A catalogue of the Calouste Gulbenkian collection of Greek coins*. 1: *Italy, Sicily, Carthage, Lissabon*

Sambon, A, 1903 *Les monnaies antiques de l'Italie*, 1

Scheers, S, 1975 *Les monnaies gauloises de la collection A Danicourt à Péronne (France, Somme)*

Scheers, S, 1977a *Traité de numismatique celtique*. 2: *La Gaule Belgique* (Paris)

Scheers, S, 1977b La circulation des monnaies gauloises sur le territoire trévire, *Bulletin Antiq Luxembourgeoises*, 8, 26–32

Thompson, M, 1968 The mints of Lysimachus, in Kraay, C M, & Jenkins, G K (eds), *Essays in Greek coinage presented to Stanley Robinson*

Thompson, M, Mørkholm, O, & Kraay, C M (eds), 1973 *An inventory of Greek coin hoards*

Roman monetary impact on the Celtic world—thoughts and problems   *Richard Reece*

In a recent article Daphne Nash has made one of the first successful forays into the world of Romano-Celtic interaction as seen by coins (Nash 1978). She suggests many very important lines of thought which should have an impact on all discussions of coins in the 1st centuries BC and AD. I would pick out especially her ideas that Roman coinage is fed into civilian economies primarily by the Roman army, that in Central Gaul Celtic bronze coins played the role of the Imperial quadrans, and that the economy of Gaul is less developed than that of Rome because it needs coins of lower value than the mint of Rome commonly issued in any numbers. Her chronological survey ends, in Gaul, at the time of the invasion of Britain, and it is extremely interesting to me that the story in Britain seems to continue from the point reached in Gaul rather than going through the same stages as Gaul in its own good time. Thus, in Britain, there seems to be no period like the one surveyed in Gaul where the pre-Roman coinages are left to themselves to supply everyday needs: by the mid 1st century AD non-Roman coinages were coming to an end in many parts of the west so that the conquest of Britain seems to mean the speedy end of British coinage. Daphne Nash has been able to make these suggestions on evidence which, on the archaeological side, is of very uneven quality, so that when the results of good excavations in Gaul are published we will expect from her many more deductions.

Meanwhile I want to balance up the Roman side of the picture with some information, some suggestions, and some questions. First, what do we know of the Roman use of coinage, and the people who used it; second, how fast did the use of Roman coins spread out from Rome; third, how do we recognize Roman coins in native contexts? Before attempting to answer my own questions I am going to insist on the provision of a brief background of Roman coinage, against which to see the Romano-Celtic interaction.

Rome came late to coinage if the City is judged against Magna Graecia, for the colonies of Sicily and the South of Italy were producing great silver coinages well before the end of the 6th century BC. Some of the Etruscan cities north of Rome were producing coinages in the 5th century BC, yet the earliest coinage at Rome can probably not be dated before 300 BC. The influence which produced this first coinage, and perhaps the direction in which these coins principally moved, is obvious from the first legend in which Greek, not Latin, letters are used and the weight standard, which is also Greek. After at least two centuries of trading with Greek colonies it is fair to say that Rome finally succumbed to coinage on a Greek model and with Greek trade in mind (Burnett 1977).

Roman bronze coinage as it first appears is cumbersome to say the least—great slabs of bronze with cast designs, and then cast round coins up to one Roman pound in weight. Silver in the form of didrachms was much more obviously negotiable, and the development of the Roman silver coinage in volume of production, and its distribution, goes hand in hand with the military effort of the 3rd century BC culminating in victory in the Punic wars.

With Italy mainly subdued and Sicily conquered, the Greek influence on the Roman coinage was removed and a purely Roman coinage was established on the basis of the bronze as, its bronze sub-divisions, and its silver multiples such as the denarius (10 asses). From the introduction of this coinage in c 213 BC a pattern was laid down which lasted for two centuries during which the main coin to be produced was the silver denarius. Gold had been produced

for one short time around 209 BC, but this rare issue stood alone in the Roman coinage until the time of Sulla (80 BC). Crawford (1974, 633) has been able to compare the yearly production of silver coinage with the size of the army and, although the correlation for some years is not good, there is certainly a demonstrable link between the number of soldiers needing pay and the number of denarii struck. But the period of Roman coinage which most concerns us here is the period from about 80 BC to AD 80, the period when Romano-Celtic interaction was highest.

In one way the coinage from Sulla to Titus (AD 80) was commendably static; the silver denarius fluctuated a little in weight and fineness but it was the basic coin in the economy both before and after these dates. Crawford's work on Republican denarii and the army (Crawford 1974, 694) ties in with Daphne Nash's suggestion that Celtic silver is for payment of troops in Gaul and the great issues of Marc Antony on the eve of the battle of Actium, and the provincial issues of Augustus all fit in with this idea. Later in the Empire progressive complication of the coinage makes any such simple link more difficult to demonstrate in detail.

Sulla is a good person with whom to begin any period of uniformity for it is with the disbandment of his armies that gold coins find a permanent foothold in the Roman scheme, and this was confirmed by the triumvirs and codified by Augustus. But if gold coinage can be said to develop in this period—and it is perhaps worth noting that Roman gold coinage grows dramatically under Caesar as Celtic gold coinage declines—our chosen 160-year span has two major irregularities. The denarius as a coin was reasonably regular; after the reign of Augustus its volume of production was not. Bronze coinage at this time was, to say the least, erratic. The late Republic saw the minting of very little bronze coinage though in theory there was available the old Republican system from the as to the uncia (12 to the as). Most of the Mediterranean area had its own answer to this with local coinage—Asia Minor, North Africa, Spain, Greece—and the Celtic world formed an acceptable part of this pattern. Rome attempted some bronze coinages after about 60 BC, but in very small supplies, and it was left to Augustus to set out the imperial system of bronze sestertii (4 to the denarius), dupondii (2 asses), asses (4 to the sestertius), semisses and quadrantes (half- and quarter-as). Thenceforward the system was settled, but the mint production was, as for denarii, highly changeable. Under Claudius, for example, at a crucial period in the archaeology of Britain and Germany little gold and practically no silver was produced; bronze seems to have started the reign well but tailed off severely by AD 50. Under Nero silver continued rare, gold was also rare, and bronze was not struck from 54 to 64 when a great mint reorganization loosed a stream of coinage in all metals.

This may seem to be a Roman numismatist talking about the system he knows because he either knows nothing else or is afraid to venture out of his own field. There are better reasons for the details that I have set down and they concern the nature and the composition of the coinage with which the Celts had to come to terms. The Roman coinage seldom had either the opportunity or the inclination to be equally up-to-date or relevant to local requirements in all its denominations at once. Thus late in the reign of Tiberius, in the reign of Caligula, or early in the reign of Claudius, new silver was apparently seldom seen. Denarii of the Republic and Augustus made up the deficiency, and the few Roman coins buried in a hoard predominantly of Celtic silver coins have therefore very little chronological value. A hoard of Celtic bronze coins was the equivalent perhaps of a hoard of Roman quadrantes. Few, if any, quadrantes occur in hoards of Celtic bronze, but this is not because of a 'war of currencies' or 'the conservative taste of the Celts', it is because quadrantes were issued only intermittently and even then travelled rarely outside Italy. As low denominations, halved asses were more common in Germany than in Italy, Cyrenaica, Spain, and Narbonensis, where, as Daphne Nash points out, whole Roman coins were more common in circulation anyway (Nash, 1978, 25). These points, though pedestrian, can be vital to a proper understanding of Romano-Celtic interaction, and I shall return to them later.

Can we answer the question of how these Roman coins were used and who used them? There are three rays of light: the sacred, the profane, and the sewer. There is one great source on coin use in Rome in the early Empire, the *Satyricon*, a picaresque narrative probably by the aristocrat Petronius and probably therefore written at the court of Nero (Appendix A). All the coins of the Augustan monetary system are referred to at least once, but never in passages of poetry, pseudo-philosophy, or history: they are mentioned by the low, the vulgar, and the poor as they chat or boast or just pass the time of day. Sums of money are in the conversation of the well-off, just as they are in the works of the historian Tacitus—someone married a cool million, another has scarcely half a million of his three million inheritance left—but coins only concern the lower end of society. They use dupondii to buy lupin seeds, asses to buy large loaves of bread; if their wives make an as they get a semis; hangers-on may get dinners from their patrons worth two denarii; and gold pieces need to be sewn into the hems of shirts to keep them safe; the quadrans, however, usually ends up in the sweepings on the muck-heap, whence a particularly miserly person might be seen to extract it with his teeth.

The sacred ray of light comes from the Gospels (Appendix B). This may sound intimidating but is in fact relatively painless. The late John Morris, a firm non-believer, was equally firm about the value of the Gospels as a historical source on lower-class life; no other literary source confirms the civilian duty to carry a soldier's pack for a mile when commanded, certainly none suggests 'go with him two miles'. References to the physical use of coins are in just the vein that we have already recognized in the *Satyricon*. Their distribution in the four Gospels and *Acts* is instructive, for the three synoptic gospels (Matthew, Mark, Luke) contain all the references of value. The gospel of John is interpretative and might not be expected to be of great use here, but *Acts* is narrative and, although it should be of use, there is very little reward for a thorough search. This pinpoints the references, for they are predominantly in reported speech in the actual sayings of Jesus, collections of which some New Testament scholars have seen as the earliest written sources for the Gospel compilation. These sayings give a firm impression of a religious leader speaking to the lower stratum of society about topics which will be of immediate interest to them. The loss of a silver coin which must be found, agreement over the daily wage of one denarius, debt being extracted to the uttermost quadrans, two sparrows sold for an as (or is it five for two asses'—Matthew versus Luke), and the only reference in ancient literature to anyone actually looking at a coin—whose is this image and inscription? This is coinage in use in an eastern province, and it is remarkably Romanized for the late 20s AD, for the denominations are not peculiar to the Latin translation but are firmly based in the earliest Greek texts.

Finally there is the Cloaca Maxima. This must be one of the sources for the general finds of coins which were made when the Tiber was straightened, dredged, and entravertined at the end of the 19th century as part of Rome's rejuvenation to become the Italian capital. The coins are most easily accessible in my published paper (Reece 1973); I reproduce the earliest coins here for ease of reference:

	Sestertii	Dupondii and asses	Semisses and quadrantes
Augustus–Gaius	136	2 395	64
Claudius	90	578	17
Nero–Vitellius	65	124	13
Vespasian–Domitian	118	625	3

Two accusations of bias have been made against this material; first that as it has not been excavated from a known site we do not know how it come to be a group, so we do not know what the bias may be; second, that in the actual finding small coins may have been disregarded, or simply not found or kept. Few sites in and around Rome have been excavated with perfect method, although we now have coin lists from a few villa sites in which can have confidence, and from the work at Ostia. The representation of denominations on these sites is similar to that of the Tiber finds and this encourages me to use them. The evidence from the Tiber is also congruent, as we shall see with the evidence from the texts, and this again seems a point in favour of its use.

Bearing in mind these criticisms it seems that, even in the centre of the Empire, in the lowest rubbish levels the smallest change is very scarce. This does not mean that it was little used, for what little was issued may have been intensively used before loss. But proportions of coins lost must reflect the numbers of coins in circulation in some way, and the loss in the Tiber, bias ignored, was predominantly of asses and dupondii. This ties in with both the Gospels and the *Satyricon*. All the evidence combines to suggest that the smallest change was too small for general use—the quadrans on the muck-heap, the widow's half-quadrans, the uttermost quadrans, the 37 asses for every quadrans lost. And, in Rome at least, no mention that this is at all unsatisfactory. The widow's mite perhaps suggests that the eastern provinces, like Gaul, could use smaller coins than the as.

We have looked briefly at the Roman system in theory, and the Roman system in use; how did that system spread? A detailed answer may be found in Dr John Kent's recent article (Kent 1973). Here I want only to give a very quick sketch based on an idea of Harold Mattingly (1978) and material of Michael Crawford (1969; 1977). The hoards of Roman Republican coins, as collected by Crawford, can be plotted on a map taking note of the spread of the hoards according to the period in which the coins were struck. The periods into which the coinage has been grouped, and the areas which hoards cover at any given period are given on the map, Fig 10 (drawn by Simon James).

At first the pre-denarius coinage was confined to Italy, the islands, and perhaps Spain. Expansion of Roman rule is preceded by growing trade contacts to the South of France, Spain, and then North Africa, Jugoslavia, Romania, the Black Sea, and Greece. By 45 BC hoards containing Republican coins were common in the west Mediterranean and the Balkans, and the contour stretches into Gaul and southern Germany. Only by the reign of Augustus are France, the Netherlands, and the Rhine engulfed. And Britain remained outside. From this very rough sketch I want to extract only two points which will bring us full circle in the problems of Romano-Celtic interaction. The map concentrates on hoards; site finds are useless for the purpose, for they cannot generally be dated. The purpose

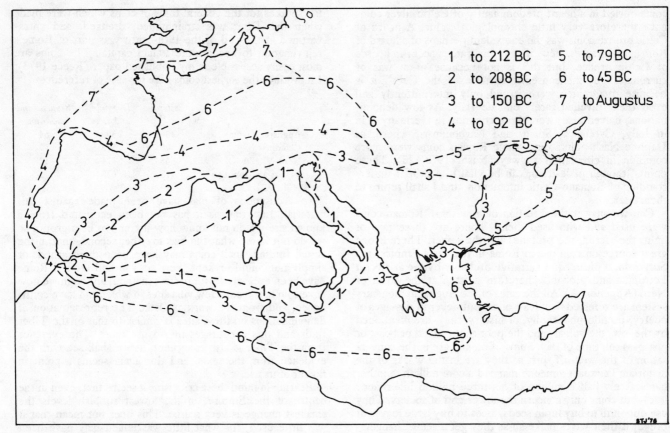

Fig 10 Roman Republican coin hoards

of hoards of Roman coins in the Celtic world is far from obvious.

The second point may be taken first, for Crawford has recently looked at one aspect of Roman coin hoards in barbarian Romania (Crawford 1977). Here, as the map makes clear, the coin hoards not only considerably antedate any direct Roman political influence north of the Danube, but they also do not have a continuous history. Crawford sees this isolated episode of coin transfer as payment for slaves. This example must warn us that the flag is just as likley to follow trade as the other way round. More simply, though Republican denarii and the Roman army are closely connected, and while the presence of the army may mean the presence of denarii, denarii travel into the Celtic world for many different reasons beyond military campaigns.

In the present state of archaeological knowledge this sort of study must rely on hoards, for they can usually be dated by the sequence of coins in them. But not even all hoards are secure. Crawford (1969, 109, no 343) gives the French Compreignac hoard in his section on hoards of 78–49 BC because the latest Republican denarius belongs to the mid 50s. Daphne Nash (1978, no 23) mentions that this hoard contains 'Gallic issues . . . of the forties', and therefore the Republican issues cannot be used to date the hoard. The Republican coins seem to be in proper sequence, and the Republican hoard encapsulated in the Celtic hoard does indeed therefore belong to the mid 50s. My point is not one of reproof to Crawford, for he has said nothing wrong, it is of warning to others; because of the stability of the denarius coinage up to the reign of Trajan, it is often unsafe for use in close dating.

In the best of all possible worlds all coins would be found in an archaeological context in relation to other coins, to pottery, and to other datable objects. Where the context of Republican coins found in Britain is known it has always, so far, been in a context which must be dated after AD 43. Single finds, or small numbers of Republican coins buried with British coins, cannot be used to give a pre-conquest date. I am not denying that coins of the Republic entered the Celtic world in Britain before AD 43; Simone Scheers has demonstrated that they must have been there for British die engravers to copy in issues which followed Republican models. What I want to insist on is scrupulous attention to detail in the recording of the context of any pre-Roman coin in Britain and on the continent so that we may build up a proper corpus of Romano-Celtic interaction. When this corpus is interpreted against the rather difficult background of the Roman coinage of the time we shall be able to solve our problems and refine our thoughts, and be ready to talk about the Roman monetary impact on the Celtic world.

Appendix A: Coins in the Satyricon

References are to the numbered chapters of the text (Loeb text with translation by M Heseltine: revised edn 1969)

Aureus
13 A shirt with aurei sewn safely into it
30 The steward sitting in the atrium counting aurei
33 Gold and silver denarii used as counters in a board game
44 An aedile who accepted bribes of 1 000 aurei
76 A wife who sold all her gold bangles and provided her husband with 100 aurei
137 Two aurei to the peasant whose goose has been accidentally killed, to keep her quiet

Denarius
45 The dinner which will be given to me and my family will only be worth 2 denarii
57 Trimalchio paid 1 000 denarii for his freedom
67 A slave who snores and is cross-eyed, but he is just like Venus, cost 300 denarii
79 The dinner Trimalchio gave to all comers cost two denarii a head

109   A forfeit for 'pursuing' the hero—200 denarii each time
109   A forfeit for pursuing the hero's boy friend—100 denarii each time

Sestertium (= 1 000 or 10 000 sestertii??)
38   Ten (?sestertium)—a fortune he had and lost
38   Eighty (?sestertium)—the fortune of a freedman
43   A hundred (?sestertium)—the fortune left by a freedman
53, 74, 76, 141   A hundred sestertium, translates as 'a million'—put back in the strong box one day for lack of investments, Trimalchio could have married a million, lost in one shipwreck, a legacy
117   Two hundred—another loss by shipwreck
45, 71, 76, 88, 117   Three hundred—a legacy and only half a million left, a man who started from nothing made this, another loss by shipwreck, vowed to the Capitoline temple if the venture succeeds, a fortune in Africa

Sestertius
30   The steward's clothes were worth scarcely ten sestertii
65   A freedman left 50 000 sestertii when he died
45   *Gladiatores sestertiarii*—worthless—they would have fallen over if you had blown on them
45   Glyco, *sestertiàrius homo*—silly man—gave his steward to fight the beasts

Dupondius
14   A dupondius with which to buy lupin seeds to eat
58   No one is worth a dupondius
58   When I get going I don't care a dupondius for my own mother
58   *Dominus dupundiarius*—your worthless master
74   And I, *homo dipundiarius*—silly man—could have married a million

As
8   A room in a brothel for an as
43   He started from an as and made good (see Quadrans)
44   An aedile who didn't care an as for our lives
44   The bread that you could buy for an as was more than you and a mate could eat
57   I owe no one a brass as (brass farthing)
61   She made an as, and she gave me a semis
77   Believe me, if you have only an as to your name that's how people will value you

Semis
61   She made an as and she gave me a semis

Quadrans
43   He started from an as and [was so careful] he would pick up a quadrans out of the muck-heap with his teeth

Aes
14   Recover our treasure cheaply *(parvo aere)*
58   I can do sums in small change *(ad aes)*, weights *(ad pondum)*, and money *(ad nummum)*
140   Where would pickpockets be without boxes or purses jingling with small change?

Nummus
14   To sell the truth for coins—money
37   She counts coin by the corn measure
37   Trimalchio, *nummorum nummos*, money bag of money bags (??)
43   He left a million–*omnia in nummis*—all in hard cash
44   An aedile got more in bribes in one day than he inherited
71   Trimalchio in splendour on his tomb doling out money from a sack
97   A reward, *nummos mille*—a thousand pieces
137   He who has money sails through life securely
137   If you have money every wish will come true

Nummularius
56   The moneychanger who *per argentum aes videt*—can see the bronze in the silver-plated coin

Pecunia
14   What can laws do where money reigns?
15   Our money returned to us
58   Let's go to the forum and borrow money
88   No one need be ashamed of wanting money
107   If they had taken your money . . .

Pondus
58   Sums in weights and measures (see Aes)
67   Fortunata has on her six and a half pounds of gold
88   Even senators promise a thousand pounds of gold to Jupiter if all goes well

Appendix B: Coins and money in the New Testament

Quadrans   Matt 5, 26: debt claimed to the uttermost quadrans
Mark 12, 42: the widow's donation of two minuta, which is a quadrans

Minutum (in Greek *lepton*) Mark 12, 42 as above
Luke 12, 59: debt claimed to the uttermost minutum
Luke 21, 2: the widow's two minuta

As   Matt 10, 29: two sparrows sold for an as

Dipondius (in Greek *assarion duo*) Luke 12, 6: five sparrows sold for a dipondius

Drachma   Luke 15, 8: if you have ten drachmae and lose one you will search for it

Didrachma   Matt 17, 24: for the payment of taxes

Denarius   Matt 22, 19; Mark 12, 15; Luke 20, 24: they showed him the denarius for paying the tax
Matt 18, 28; Luke 7, 41: debts of 50, 100, and 500 denarii
Luke 10, 35: the good samaritan leaves two denarii for the victim of attack
Mark 14, 5; John 12, 5: the ointment Mary Magdalene uses could have been sold for 300 denarii
Mark 6, 37; John 6, 7: 200 denarii would not buy bread to feed the 5 000
Matt 20, 1–16: the labourers in the vineyard agree for a denarius a day
Revelation 6, 6: a denarius for a quart of wheat or three quarts of barley—famine prices
(in Greek *argyrion*) Acts 19, 19: the cost of the magic books burnt, 50 000 denarii

Argenteus (in Greek *argyrion*) Matt 26, 15; 27, 3: the thirty pieces of silver for Judas's betrayal

Stater   Matt 17, 27: which turned up in the mouth of the fish to pay taxes

Aes (in Greek *kerma*) John 2, 15: Jesus upset the small change on the tables of the moneychangers
(in Greek *chalkon*) Mark 6, 8: the apostles should not take small change or money on their preaching journeys

Aurum   Matt 10, 9: as above, nor gold

Argentum   Matt 10, 9: as above, nor silver

Talenta   Matt 18, 24: the debt of ten thousand talents compared with 100 denarii
Matt 25, 15: the parable of the talents, 5, 2, and one

Mna   Luke 19, 13: the parable of the talents expressed as mnas (? 100 denarii)

Pecunia (in Greek *chalkon*) Matt 10, 9: sending out the apostles— no money
(in Greek *argyrion*) Luke 9, 3: as above
Matt 25, 18; Matt 25, 27; Luke 19, 15; Luke 19, 23: The parable of the talents—one servant went away with the money, the Lord called for the people to whom he had given the money, and asked why they had not put it out ad mensam (to the moneychangers)
Matt 28, 12: the guards at the tomb were given a lot of money *(pecuniam copiosam)*
Mark 14, 11; Luke 22, 5: the priests promised to give Judas money
(in Greek *time*) Acts 19, 19: when they totted up how much the burned books were worth . . . 50 000 denarii
(in Greek *chremata*) Acts 8, 18: Simon Magus was impressed by the apostles' gifts and offered them pecunia *(chremata)* for them. Peter said may you and your pecunia *(argyrion)* go to . . .
Acts 24, 26: Felix had hopes of a bribe from Paul

Tributus (in Greek *phoros*) Luke 20, 22: Should we pay tribute to Caesar?
(in Greek *kensos*) Mark 12, 14: as above

Census (in Greek *nomisma tou kensou*) Matt 22, 17–19: Show me the tribute coin

Pretium (in Greek *chrema*) Acts 4, 37: They sold the field and put the sum at the Apostles' feet
(in Greek *times argyriou*) Acts 7, 16: Abraham bought the tomb for a sum of silver

Stipendium (in Greek *opsonion*) Luke 3, 14: Soldiers be satisfied with your pay

Imago (in Greek *icon*) Matt 22, 20; Mark 12, 16; Luke 20, 24: Whose is the image on the coin and they said Caesar's

Superscriptio (in Greek *epigraphe*) Matt 22, 20; Mark 12, 16; Luke 20, 24: Whose is the image and superscription? (Mark and Luke use *inscriptio*)

Nummularius (in Greek *kollybiston*) Matt 21, 12; Mark 11, 15; John 2, 15: The tables of the moneychangers overturned (John includes aes)
(in Greek *trapezites*) Matt 25, 27: The talents which should have been at the moneychangers to earn interest

Bibliography

Burnett, A, 1977 The coinages of Rome and Magna Graecia in the late
   fourth and early third centuries BC, *Swiss Numis Rev*, **56,** 92–121
Crawford, M, 1969 *Roman Republican coin hoards*
Crawford, M, 1974 *Roman Republican coinage*
Crawford, 1977 Republican denarii in Romania: the suppression of piracy
   and the slave trade, *J Roman Stud*, **67,** 117–24
Kent, J P C, 1973 *Cercle des études numismatiques* (jan-mars 1973), 2ff
Mattingly, H, 1978 Review of Crawford 1974, in *Antiq J*, **57,** 37
Nash, D, 1978 Plus ça change — currency in Central Gaul from Julius
   Caesar to Nero, in Carson R A G, & Kraay, C M (eds), *Scripta
   Nummaria Romana*, 12–31
Reece, R, 1973 Roman coinage in the western Empire, *Britannia*, **4,**
   227–51

Nearly 40 years ago, in April 1940, Derek Allen presented his now-classic paper 'The Belgic dynasties of Britain and their Coins' before a meeting of the Society of Antiquaries in London (Allen 1944). In it he set out to construct a history of the late pre-Roman Iron Age of Britain, based on a geographical, stylistic, and chronological study of the surviving coinage. This work, with periodic updatings, has remained a standard part of subsequent considerations of the British Iron Age. The CBA Conference on the Problems of the Iron Age in Southern Britain, held in London in 1958, provided Allen with the opportunity to reappraise the origins of coinage in Britain (Allen 1961). His considered views, stated with great clarity, were readily accepted by subsequent writers (Frere 1967; Hawkes 1968; Cunliffe 1974), all of whom found that his historical approach provided a satisfactory model against which to consider the rest of the archaeological evidence. One should, however, call to mind Allen's perceptive warning: 'It is essential in interpreting coin evidence to recall constantly that it is only part, and not always the most important part, of the historical record' (Allen 1961, 98).

The historical approach to coinage has continued to develop. Rodwell's detailed restudy of the coinage of south-eastern Britain extends and refines the arguments, presenting a meticulously argued 'history' for the period based substantially on changes in coin type and distribution (Rodwell 1976), while the work of Simone Scheers in France and the Low Countries uses historical events as a framework for understanding the coinage (Scheers 1972; 1977). The historical model is further examined in the recent work of John Kent (Kent 1978a and below, pp 40–2).

Whilst the historical approach thus continues to thrive, the vogue for discovering and analysing economic systems in archaeology, which developed in the 1960s, led some writers to focus attention on the potential of the coin evidence in studies of this kind (Collis 1971a; 1971b; 1974; Haselgrove 1976). The writer, by virtue of his early archaeological training, must confess to being more in sympathy with this school of thought. The present paper, however, is an attempt to consider the quality of the data against the broad social questions which might reasonably be asked of it, rather than to engage in the polemic which surrounds model building whether historical or economic.

The nature of the evidence

Before we can begin we must briefly consider the nature of the available data. In all some 12 624 Iron Age coins are recorded from Britain. Probably less than 50% survive today. Of this impressive total *c* 3 100 come from the single 'hoard' found at Hengistbury and a further 5 200+ from other hoards. A mere 1 100+ have been found in excavations (the majority come from three sites: Camulodunum, Braughing, and Harlow), and of these a substantial proportion are unstratified. Furthermore, it is estimated that of the 5 000 or so coins recorded on the Index housed in the Institute of Archaeology, Oxford, about two-thirds are without precise provenance.

Thus it must be realized at the outset that the data have widely varying levels of reliability. To a numismatist dealing with metrology, typology, die linking, etc, the data are of reasonable quality but to an archaeologist working with distribution patterns they are far from adequate. Not only is

most of the sample unusable because of lack of locational detail, it is also regionally biased by the many factors affecting discovery, and worse still, it is distorted to an unknown extent by the unscrupulous who wish to please collectors (including museums) by providing false find spots for material which is either without a sound location or was acquired and dispersed under dubious circumstances (Rodwell, below, pp 43–52). While distribution maps can quite reasonably be used in generalizing arguments, to attempt to use them too precisely to generate sophisticated models can give rise only to a spurious and misleading impression of accuracy.

Where individual site finds are concerned we are in even more difficulty. It is only in recent excavations like those at the temples of Harlow and Hayling or the urban sites of Braughing, Colchester, and Canterbury that reliable data are at last being provided. The distorting effects which these collections have on our maps is a firm reminder of the inadequacy of much of the rest of the record. This is not intended to be a counsel of despair but a warning that we should not ask of the data questions which, in full knowledge of their limitations, they cannot be expected reliably to answer. In the following pages we will therefore use the evidence of the coinage at a general, rather than too specific, a level.

Britain and the Continent, *c* 120–50 BC

Most scholars will agree that coinage was introduced into Britain during the period 120–50 BC, but the economic and social situation in the south-east of the country, and in particular the differences in the different regional systems, are seldom taken into account. Some aspects of these problems have been dealt with recently elsewhere (Cunliffe 1976; 1978a) but several points deserve mention here. Foremost is the fact that in the early part of the period the south-east of Britain can be divided into two distinct regions: a hillfort-dominated zone stretching from Kent and Sussex westwards to Wessex and the Cotswolds, and an area of open settlement occupying the Thames Valley, East Anglia, and the Midlands. This same division is emphasized by a consideration of the ceramics of the area. Clearly, two separate socio-economic systems are implied. In both zones coinage was adopted and a full-scale market economy eventually developed.

To suggest however that the idea of coinage in its various manifestations was completely novel might prove to be misleading. Widespread use of currency bars appears on present evidence to have preceded the introduction of coinage (if overlapping with it), while the discovery at several sites (including Winklebury and Danebury) of well made stone weights implies that careful measurement was being practised. It may well be that salt packed in ceramic containers formed another unit of value (Cunliffe 1977; 214), while the possibility that storage pits for grain may have been dug to a series of size standards is a further reminder that accurate measurement, in the interests of exchange, may have been widespread. To this we might perhaps add that some at least of the large numbers of Greek coins found in south-eastern Britain are likely to be genuine Iron Age imports, thus familiarizing the natives with the idea of the coin as a unit of value. In other words, at the time when large-scale long-distance trade was re-established in the first half of the 1st century BC, it is

Fig 11 Britain and the Continent showing the most convenient points of contact: ■ ports of trade, ○ Armorican coins, ● Gallo-Belgic coins

reasonable to assume that the communities of the south-east already practised an ordered economy in which measurement by weight and possibly by volume formed an essential part. In such circumstances the ready adoption of coinage need occasion no surprise nor would it be exceptional if a money economy were to develop soon after.

Pre-Caesarian contact

Two principal axes of contact between Britain and the Continent seem to have developed in the decades before Caesar's invasions in 55 and 54 BC. Not surprisingly, the routes chosen spanned the shortest sea crossings, requiring

the traveller to spend a minimum of time out of easy reach of land (Fig 11). One axis linked the western seaways, via Armorica, to central southern Britain, and the other lay between northern France and the Low Countries (Belgica) and the Thames estuary.

Evidence for the western axis, between Armorica and Hengistbury Head, has recently been discussed by the writer in some detail (Cunliffe 1978b) and need not detain us here. Suffice it to say that there is ample archaeological evidence for widespread trade involving the importation of pottery from Armorica and wine from Italy in exchange for which metals are the most evident of the possible British exports. Apart from the establishment of what can

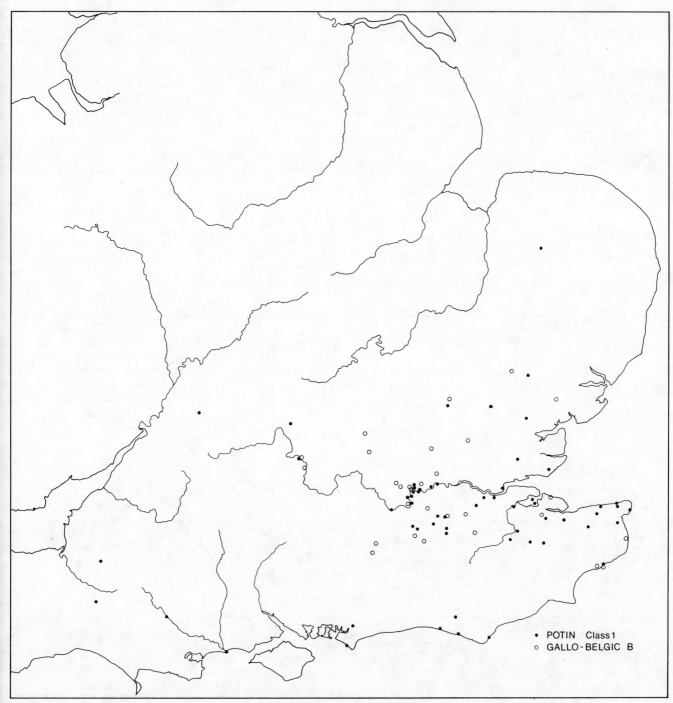

Fig 12 Distribution of Gallo-Belgic B and Potin 1 coins mapped after Allen 1961 and Haselgrove 1978

reasonably be regarded as a port-of-trade at Hengistbury and a general improvement in pottery technology in the south-west of Britain (probably involving the introduction of the potter's wheel), the trading axis had little lasting effect on the socio-economic structure of the Iron Age communities of southern Britain.

From the point of view of the present discussion it is the numismatic aspect of the contact that is of interest. It is represented by 60 or so imported Armorican coins scattered over central southern England of which 25 come from Hengistbury, a distribution sufficient in itself to imply some form of contact even if no other evidence had been available. That the subsequent local coinages owe little, apart from adherence to a silver standard, to imported

Armorican types, but instead develop from Gallo-Belgic models introduced from eastern Britain, strongly suggests that Armorican coins in Britain represented little more than valued items of precious metal: they do not seem to reflect the introduction of a new trading system based on money economy. The fact that the socio-economic system, as exemplified by the continued development of hillforts, appears to remain unchanged is a further indication that trade with Armorica had little lasting effect on southern Britain. The reasons for this are obscure. The contact could have been (and indeed probably was) short-lived, but of equal importance may have been the fact that the economic and social systems in the area were not, at this time, sufficiently structured to allow the easy adoption of the new

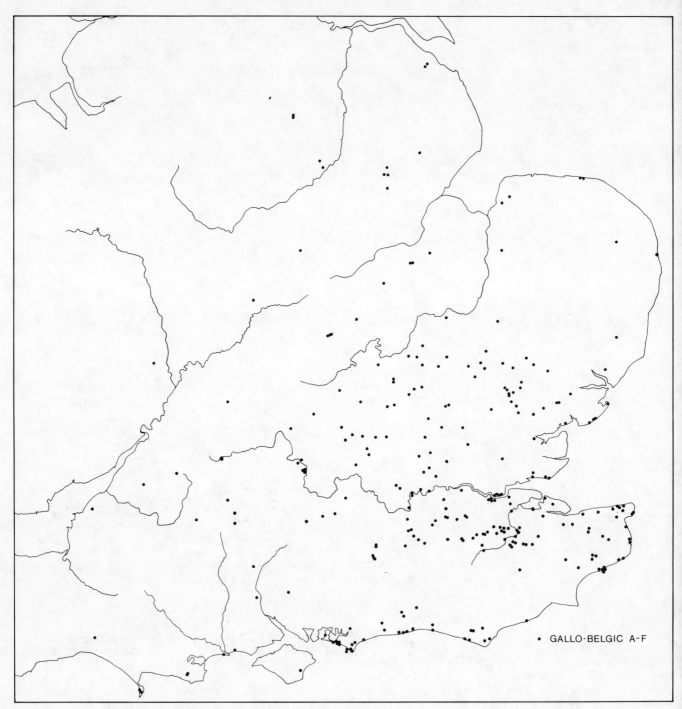

Fig 13 Distribution of Gallo-Belgic A-F coins (after Allen 1961 and Haselgrove 1978)

GALLO-BELGIC A-F

exchange system. The Armorican contact seems, then, to provide an interesting example of one of the many kinds of relationship, involving the transference of coins, which may have existed between communities.

The relationship between the Belgic territories and eastern Britain was quite different but in view of the current discussions concerning the chronology of the Gallo-Belgic coin series (Kent 1978a) it is unwise to argue the sequence of events too closely. Most writers are agreed, however, that Gallo-Belgic B coins were probably in use in Britain in the decades before Caesar's conquest, and some of the Gallo-Belgic A examples may well have been in circulation in this period. The distribution of Gallo-Belgic B centres upon the Thames estuary favouring Kent, a distri-

bution pattern very similar to that of the Potin I coinage for which Allen has argued a pre-conquest date. Mapped together (Fig 12) the gross distribution of Gallo-Belgic B and Potin I probably reflects the territory within which coinage first came into regular use in Britain. The Potin coinage is of particular interest for not only was it minted in Britain but its very existence must surely imply a system of currency involving two denominations. Collis has found it difficult to accept that potin represents small change in a money economy (Collis 1974), but Rodwell has countered his arguments (1976, 207–8). While the matter is still open to debate, particularly in view of the uncertainty of the dating evidence, we can tentatively suggest that the earliest development of British coinage took place in Kent and that

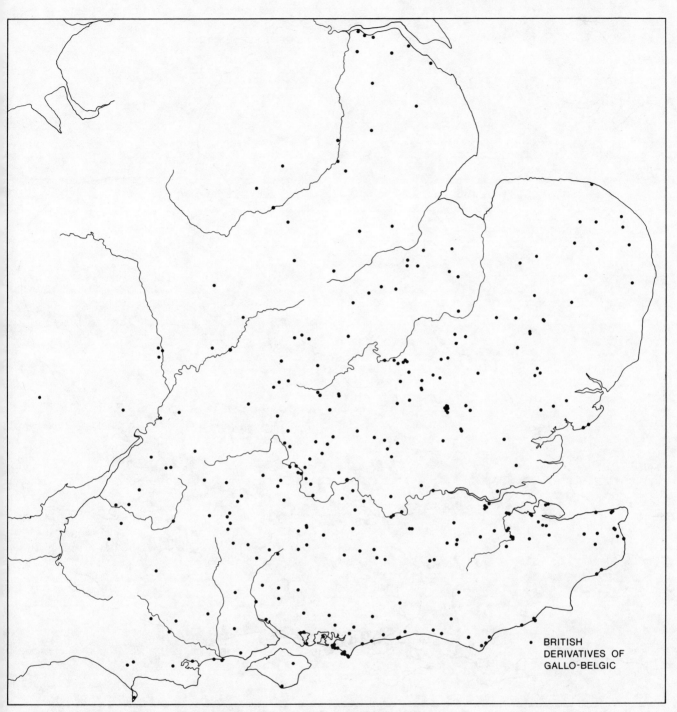

Fig 14 Distribution of British derivatives of Gallo-Belgic coins (after Allen 1961 and Haselgrove 1978)

BRITISH
DERIVATIVES OF
GALLO-BELGIC

before the Caesarian invasions coins of two value standards were in circulation. This need not imply a fully developed market economy but it is in striking contrast to the broadly contemporary situation in central southern Britain.

The reason for the contrast presumably lies in the different level of social and economic development in the two regions at the stage when contact with the Continent intensified, the communities of Kent being ready to accept and develop the new economic system. It may be that the small-scale immigration, which Caesar implies had taken place some time before his invasion, helped to intensify the rate of social change creating a climate favourable to the acceptance of a money economy.

It is reasonable to ask, if in the archaeological evidence from Kent it is possible to recognize any trace of the four kingdoms to which Caesar refers. The sites of Canterbury, Rochester, Loose, and Oldbury could have been centres at this stage but, apart from an impressive number of early Potin coins from Rochester, which are suggestive of the site's early importance, there is little satisfactory evidence yet available. The one point that does emerge from the distribution map is the concentration of coins in London to the west of the Roman city. The possibility of an oppidum in the region should not be overlooked (Kent 1978b).

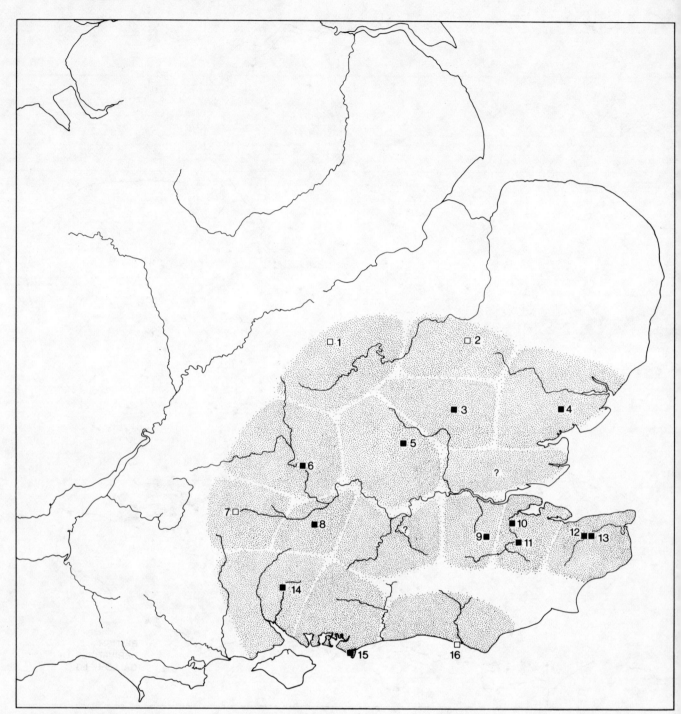

Fig 15 *Map indicating tentative socio-economic zones in the period 50 BC–AD 10. Black squares are nucleated settlements with some evidence of urban function: open squares are possible nucleated settlements.* **1** *Duston,* **2** *Cambridge,* **3** *Braughing,* **4** *Colchester,* **5** *Verulamium,* **6** *Dyke Hills,* **7** *Marlborough,* **8** *Silchester,* **9** *Oldbury,* **10** *Rochester,* **11** *Loose,* **12** *Bigbury,* **13** *Canterbury,* **14** *Winchester,* **15** *Selsey,* **16** *Castle Hill*

The effects of Caesar's Gallic Wars, 58–51 BC

Caesar's campaigns in Gaul in the decade 60–50 BC inevitably caused widespread disruption to the social and economic systems in force among the Gallic communities. Although his campaigns in Britain were by comparison of minor significance, his presence here and the close proximity of the war in Gaul cannot have failed to have dislocated tribal economies and government.

Scheers has convincingly argued that the uniface staters of the Ambiani (Gallo-Belgic E) were minted after 58 BC to facilitate the resistance of the Belgic Confederacy (Scheers

1972). Thus the appearance of these coins in Britain must belong to the Caesarian period or later. The discussion has been further extended by Kent (1978a), who has hinted that all the Gallo-Belgic coins in Britain with the exception of Gallo-Belgic B may have arrived during the Gallic War or its aftermath. If this attractive hypothesis proves to be true, the gross distribution of the Gallo-Belgic coinage in Britain should reflect in general terms the extent of the territory over which the war had its effects, allowing for the later drift of the coins by subsequent exchange which will have blurred the focus of the map (Fig 13). Some communities came into direct contact with the Romans, others will have provided mercenaries to fight against

Caesar in Gaul and Britain, who may have returned with their pay, while other regions accepted refugees. All three modes of contact are attested by Caesar. However much the map (Fig 13) may have been distorted by the later (post-Caesar) movement of coins, it is a reminder that the Gallic War was directly responsible for introducing the notion of coinage to most of the tribes of south-eastern Britain.

The conquest, and the period of Romanization in Gaul consequent upon it, probably had far reaching effects on the economic system prevalent in Britain. This can be dimly recognized in the archaeological record. Trade between the Roman world and Hengistbury stopped (Peacock 1971). Kent, which one might have expected on geographical grounds to have benefited from the proximity of Rome, does not, on present evidence, appear to have enjoyed imported luxuries, but in Essex and Hertfordshire, the territory of the Trinovantes, imported goods of all kinds are found frequently occurring in rich burials (Rodwell 1976, 301–11). The overall impression is that in the aftermath of the Gallic War long-distance trade between Britain and the now-Roman world was reorganized, the allies of Caesar benefiting at the expense of his enemies. If this is indeed so it would be necessary to postulate some kind of trading monopoly between the Romans and the Trinovantes (Cunliffe 1978b, 78–80).

Whatever the cause, the fact remains that the bulk of the overseas trade in the post-Caesarian period, observable in the archaeological record, seems to have focused on the tribes of Essex. It is tempting to see them as middle-men growing rich on the movement of commodities which they controlled.

The early post-invasion period, 50 BC–AD 10

The early post-invasion period must have been a time of dramatic economic and social readjustment in those areas of Britain in direct contact with the Roman world. In terms of settlement there was a change in the south-east of England from the old system to a new situation in which large nucleated settlements, usually enclosed, sprang up at route nodes, frequently sited at important river crossings (Cunliffe 1976, 145–9). The implication would seem to be a new concern for the control of the major trade routes, these *oppida* representing the first stages in the development of a truely urban system.

In parallel, the use of coinage expanded rapidly. In a wide fringe around the area within which the Gallo-Belgic coins were distributed, British derivatives came into use over a region spreading as far west as the Jurassic ridge (Fig 14 and Allen 1962, 25). It is tempting to see this as the natural response among the outlying tribes, who had now been brought into the trading system controlled by the south-east, the derivative coins serving to facilitate exchange within the fringe territories.

In the central zone (broadly Kent, Surrey, Middlesex, Essex, and Hertfordshire) coinage evolved rapidly, eventually giving rise to a complex of dynastic issues inscribed with the names of individuals, conventionally regarded as kings (Addedomaros, Tasciovanus, Dubnovellaunus, etc.) and sometimes bearing mint marks. The picture is complicated but the principal typological and chronological arguments have been presented in detail by Rodwell (1976) and need not here concern us further. On any reading of the evidence the situation was one of rapid change and constant readjustment. Rodwell has interpreted this in terms of the struggle for power between rival leaders but there are other ways of approaching the same data. It could, for example, be argued that the apparent state of flux in the south-east

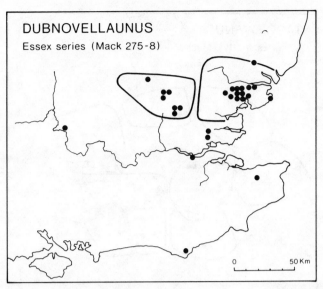

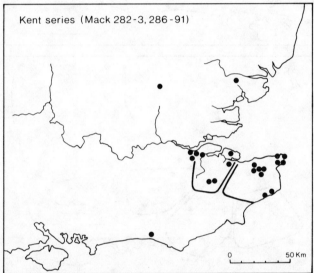

Fig 16 Distribution of coins of Dubnovellaunus (after Rodwell 1976) with tentative socio-economic zones indicated

was the result of economic and social readjustment resulting from the new economic reality brought about by the proximity of the Roman world. The gradual evolution of a money economy in the pre-Caesarian period was violently disrupted by the conquest of Gaul. It is only to be expected therefore that in the aftermath the stresses caused by the reorientation should be discernible. While these stresses may well have resulted in political manoeuvring the direct cause was more likely to have been economic.

If this possibility is admitted, we might consider ways of exploring the problem further. Theoretically one way would be to attempt to define the basic socio-economic units and to examine how, with time, these units came together into larger agglomerations sharing common coinages. The theory is difficult to put into practice but a crude attempt has been made on Fig 15 to arrive at some idea of how the map of socio-economic regions might look. It is a subjective assessment of a range of disparate evidence. Most of the regions are centred around a settlement with urban characteristics and most do reflect genuine concentrations of coins. They have been arrived at by visually comparing maps of all the British coins plotted individually. It would, of course, be possible to employ sophisticated analytical tests to examine the problem but,

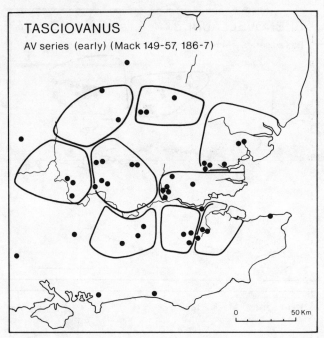

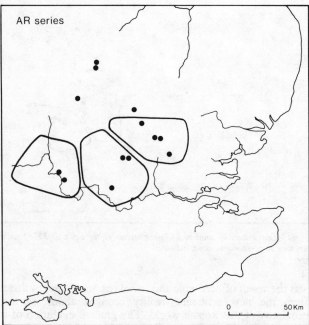

Fig 17 Distribution of certain issues of Tasciovanus (after Rodwell 1976) with tentative socio-economic zones indicated

Freed from the necessity to think within a politico-historical model, other potential explanations present themselves more easily. It could be, for example, that the gold of Tasciovanus was readily accepted for exchange purposes in the territories south of the Thames but his silver was not needed because of the availability locally of some other equivalent form of currency. Alternatively it could be that exchange across the Thames was, at this time, only of the kind requiring gold.

To generalize: socio-economic territory A might use the coins of territory B at one stage, territory C at another, and later might mint its own, or it might accept the coinages of several neighbouring territories at any one time. Further, it could be that the coinage of territory B was widely accepted in one period, occurring in a number of territories, but was unacceptable in another. In other words, it could be argued that coin distributions reflect simple economic factors and do not necessarily demonstrate political dominance. Thus the confusion in the distribution pattern, which is evident in the central area in the last four decades BC, may well represent stages in the coalescence of small socio-economic territories into larger units and the emergence of a widely accepted monetary system.

To emphasize the economic explanation as we have done should not be allowed to obscure the underlying politico-social changes which must have been taking place at this time. Some hint of this might be given by the appearance of additional names on the later coinage of Tasciovanus, Riconi, Sego, Dias, Rues, and Andoc (Rodwell 1976, 249–61). One explanation of this innovation would be to see these as representing successive partners ruling with Tasciovanus. If so, it is possible that in this coinage we see the first faltering steps in the creation of an oligarchy and with it the archaic state. Such a situation can be discerned a little earlier, towards the beginning of the century, in central Gaul where senates and magistrates replace kings and where to aspire to kingship was regarded as a crime (Nash 1976, 125–9). It is possible that a similar evolution was taking place in the central area of south-eastern Britain at the beginning of the 1st century AD.

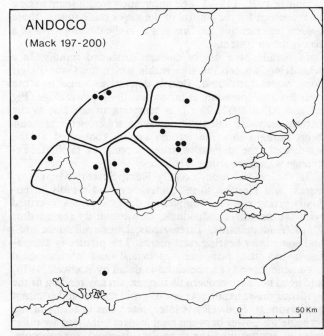

Fig 18 Distribution of ANDOC . . . coins (after Rodwell 1976), with tentative socio-economic zones indicated

bearing in mind the limitations in the nature of the evidence (above, p 29), the resulting spurious objectivity would be more dangerous than our admitted subjectivity. So long as the map is regarded more as a model than a close fit to reality it will not be misunderstood.

Such a construction does help us to consider the coin data in a new light divorced from historical argument. For example, it helps to focus on those areas where a particular issue is present, heightening the contrast with negative areas (eg Figs 16–18). It also helps to throw into sharp relief the distributional differences of the various denominations of the same dynast, most strikingly revealed when comparing the early gold of Tasciovanus with his silver issues (Fig 17).

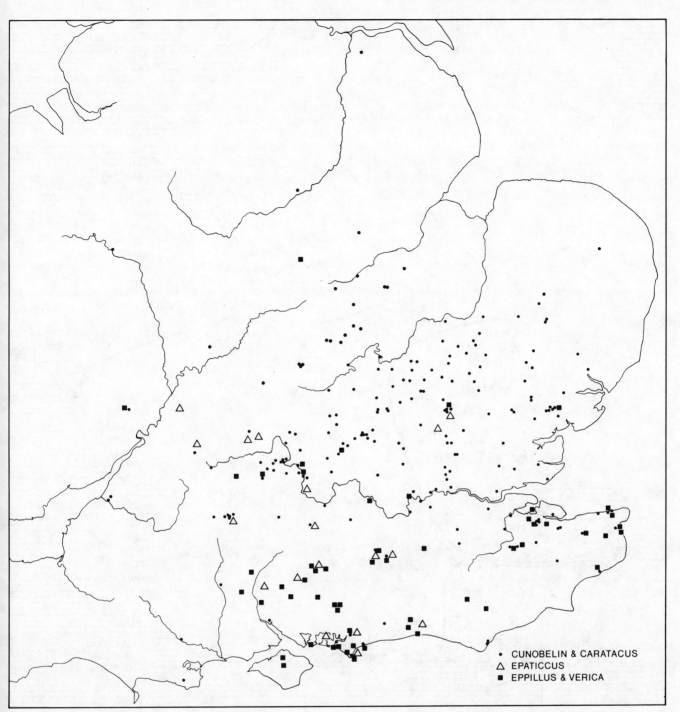

Fig 19 Distribution of coins of Cunobelin, Epaticcus, Epillus, and Verica (after Allen 1961 and Haselgrove 1978)

Legend:
- CUNOBELIN & CARATACUS
- △ EPATICCUS
- ■ EPPILLUS & VERICA

The later post-invasion period, AD 10–43

If we are correct in proposing the emergence of an oligarchy at the beginning of the 1st millennium AD, both the coin evidence and the documentary evidence would imply that the trend was short-lived, for by about AD 10 two rulers seem to have emerged to dominance: Cunobelin in the central area and Verica in the south (from the Sussex coast to the mid Thames) (Fig 19). Both rulers style themselves 'King' and both claim kinship to famous predecessors. Moreover, both are referred to as kings by Roman writers. In view of this it is difficult not to accept the continued existence of some form of monarchic rule in both areas,

though it need bear little close resemblance to that of the earlier periods.

The distribution of the coins of Cunobelin has been taken by most writers to reflect the political dominance of the king, who is frequently portrayed as a warlike aggressor intent on acquiring an empire by military expansion into neighbouring territories (Rivet 1958, fig 1). While this may be so, it is salutary to remind ourselves that there is no shred of positive archaeological or historical evidence in favour of such a view. All that we can say is that his coins circulate over a considerable area and that his minting was prolific. Allen has estimated that in his 30 years' reign no less than one million gold staters were issued (Allen 1975,

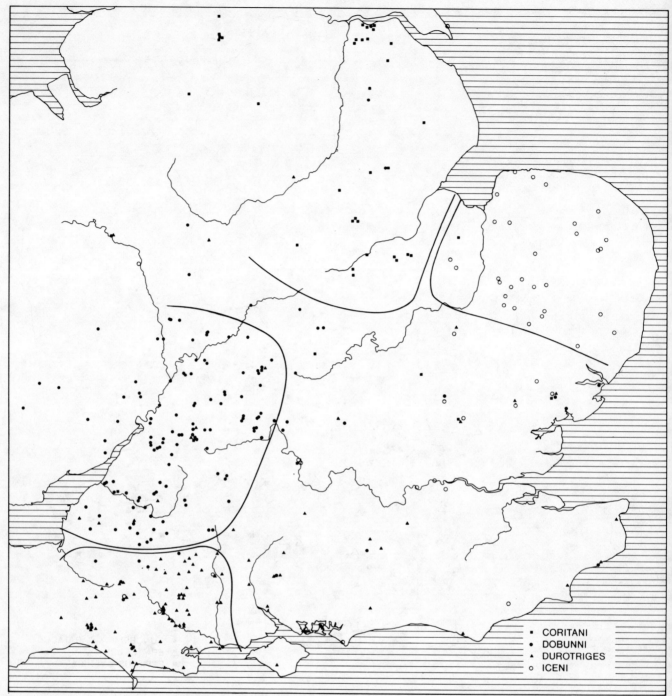

Fig 20 Distribution of coins of the peripheral tribes (after Allen 1961 and Haselgrove 1978)

4–6). The simplest explanation of these facts is that, irrespective of the extent of the territory which he ruled, Cunobelin was able to issue coins which were widely accepted over much of south-eastern Britain for the purposes of exchange and marketing. There is no reason why we should equate coin distribution with political dominance. Similarly, the coins of Verica may simply reflect the extent of the territory within which his coins were acceptable. In other words, taking the minimal view, in the last four decades or so before the invasion of AD 43 the communities of south-eastern Britain, however they were organized and whatever their political leanings, were using two basic coinages, the distribution of which shows

considerable overlapping suggesting that they were interchangeable.

A situation comparable with that outlined here could be seen to be the inevitable result of the developments in progress during the period of reorganization (50 BC–AD 10). With an increase in overseas trade and the continuing monopoly of certain communities in the south-east over this trade, a greater standardization in the coinage is only to be expected so that internal exchange, at a middleman level, could be facilitated. It is interesting that the communities of the south were still using a coinage of their own. This may well be the last remnant of the old system of independent coinages. The coinage of Verica was not extensive and issues of Cunobelin were beginning to be widely used in the south. Had native development been allowed to continue it seems probable that within a few years there would only have been one coinage in use in the south-east. The invasion of AD 43 put an end to all this.

To the west and north of the south-eastern coinage (ie that of Cunobelin and Verica) was a zone in which four systems of tribal coinage were in use: Icenian, Coritanian, Dobunnic and Durotrigian (Fig 20), each of which had developed out of one of the British derivative styles. The boundary between this fringe coinage and that of the south-east is quite distinct and shows little overlapping, a fact which might suggest that the economic system required the coins of each to circulate only within its own territory, exchange being so arranged that coins seldom crossed boundaries. Bearing in mind the distribution of raw materials in Britain, particularly metals, it will be evident that these fringe groups must have performed the function of middlemen within the trade network of the period. Their individual coinages were necessary to articulate their own internal economic systems, which will have become more complex in response to their role in the developing patterns of long distance trade.

The fringe coinages are of considerable interest in the light which, potentially, they may shed on the problems of social organization. The dual names appearing on the coins of the Coritani are highly suggestive of a system of ruling magistrates (Allen 1963, 28–32) while Allen's recent and detailed study of the coins of the Iceni is of particular interest in suggesting the existence of three distinct *pagi*, remaining in evidence even after the emergence of a tribal coinage bearing the name of the tribe (Allen 1970). The processes involved in the development of Icenian coinage may well, in microcosm, reflect those which we have suggested were in operation in the south-east in the decades following Caesar's invasion. The implication of the tribal coinages are many but are not directly relevant to the present discussion.

Concluding remarks

The story of the emergence and development of British coinage outlined all too briefly above places a different emphasis on the coin evidence to that commonly adopted by those who seek to use 'historical' explanations. It does not necessarily conflict with the historical model but it does show how tenuous and unsupported are so many of the historical assumptions. Derek Allen himself realized this when he wrote 'Any attempt to read a complete history of any people into the surviving relics of its coinage is bound to mislead: in all probability the coinage tends to reflect only the moments of prosperity and disaster' (Allen 1976, 203–4). While fully agreeing with the first sentiment the present writer is a little less pessimistic about the coin evidence as a whole. It cannot give us a reliable history but carefully studied it might be possible to discern the dynamics of change, and through this to improve our understanding of social and economic development.

Bibliography

Allen, D F, 1944 The Belgic dynasties of Britain and their coins, *Archaeologia*, **90,** 1–46
Allen, D F, 1961 The origins of coinage in Britain: a reappraisal, in Frere, S S (ed), *Problems of the Iron Age in southern Britain*, 97–308
Allen, D F, 1962 Celtic coins, in *Map of southern Britain in the Iron Age*, 19–32
Allen, D F, 1963 *The coins of the Coritani*
Allen, D F, 1970 The coins of the Iceni, *Britannia*, **1,** 1–33
Allen, D F, 1975 Cunobelin's gold, *ibid*, **6,** 1–19
Allen, D F, 1976 Wealth, money and coinage in Celtic society, in Megaw, J V S (ed), *To Illustrate the Monuments*, 199–208
Collis, J R, 1971a Functional and theoretical interpretations of British coinage, *World Archaeol*, **3,** 1, 71–84
Collis, J R, 1971b Markets and money, in Jesson, M, & Hill, D (eds), *The Iron Age and its hill-forts*, 97–104
Collis, J R, 1974 A functionalist approach to pre-Roman coinage, in Casey, J, & Reece, R (eds), *Coins and the archaeologist*, 1–11
Cunliffe, B W, 1974 *Iron Age communities in Britain*
Cunliffe, B W, 1976 The origins of urbanization in Britain, in Cunliffe & Rowley 1976, 135–62
Cunliffe, B W, 1977 Danebury, Hampshire: second interim report on the excavations, 1971–5, *Antiq J*, **56,** 198–216
Cunliffe, B W, 1978a Settlement and population in the British Iron Age: some facts, figures and fantasies, in Cunliffe, B W, & Rowley, R T (eds), *Lowland Iron Age communities in Europe*, 3–24
Cunliffe, B W, 1978b *Hengistbury Head*
Cunliffe, B W, & Rowley, R T, 1976 *Oppida: the beginnings of urbanization in barbarian Europe*
Frere, S S, 1967 *Britannia*
Haselgrove, C, 1976 External trade as a stimulus to urbanization, in Cunliffe & Rowley 1976, 25–49
Hawkes, C F C, 1968 New thoughts on the Belgae, *Antiquity*, **42,** 6–16
Kent, J P C, The origins and development of Celtic gold coinage in Britain, *Actes du Congrès International d'Archéologie: Rouen, 3, 4, 5 juillet 1975*, 313–24
Kent, J P C, 1978b The London area in the Late Iron Age: an interpretation of the earliest coins, in *Collectanea Londiniensia: studies presented to Ralph Merrifield*, 53–8
Nash, D, 1976 The growth of urban society in France, in Cunliffe & Rowley 1976, 95–133
Peacock, D P S, 1971 Roman amphorae in pre-Roman Britain, in Jesson, M, & Hill, D (eds) *The Iron Age and its hill-forts*, 161–88
Rivet, A L F, 1958 *Town and country in Roman Britain*
Rodwell, W, 1976 Coinage, oppida and the rise of Belgic power in south-eastern Britain, in Cunliffe & Rowley 1976, 181–367
Scheers, S, 1972 Coinage and currency of the Belgic tribes during the Gallic War, *Brit Numis J*, (1972), 1–6
Scheers, S, 1977 *Traité de numismatique celtique* **II**: *La Gaule Belgique*

'Coins and the origins of currency' involves an important dichotomy of concept, which my title seeks to circumvent. My terms of reference enable me to exclude the much more subtle and elusive questions of the origin of *currency* or of *money* and my remarks in this paper will be confined to those small, round, metal objects, essentially resembling coinage of the present day, which we instantly recognize as coins.

The questions we pose are three: Where? When? Why? All others are subsumed in these three. A fourth—By whom?—is really a giant red herring. It tempts, because we lie here in the penumbral zone between prehistory and history, an area in which the archaeologist and numismatist have been too prone to egg one another on to ever more inspired, or (dare one say?) audacious, 'conclusions'. Mutual disillusionment has followed often enough. In my own experience are the barren (as the events showed) controversies over the dating of 'barbarous radiates' and the Merovingian coins of Sutton Hoo: confidence is more easily shattered than established. Having established the principle that two convergent hypotheses do not confirm one another, we can agree that it is necessary in the absence of specific evidence to erect and explore (and freely discard) hypothetical chronologies of material and models of social and political structure.

'Where' is the easiest or at least the most facile problem. In 1839, when Celtic coin studies were singularly ill founded, Thomas Burgon spelled out the need for the systematic recording of coin provenances (Burgon 1839). Since then, we have exploited this very basic aid to attribution to the utmost of our bent. But, of course, find-spots reflect a pattern of disbursement and circulation, loss and concealment; they speak of origin only by further inferences, which may or may not be correct.

For early Celtic coins, 'when' is a matter of unresolved controversy, not to say conjecture. It is merely clear that the western Celts imitated Greek gold coins of the 4th and 3rd centuries BC, and that in Gaul the conclusion of the Gallic War in 51 BC marked the end of gold coinage. Colbert de Beaulieu and others have sought an intermediate fixed point in the fall of the Arvernian kingdom in 121 BC, but Dr Nash (1975) has made it painfully clear that this event has no perceptible relevance. We can with some plausibility define the coins struck in Belgic Gaul during the Gallic War; their relevance to Britain we shall discuss in due course.

'Why?' involves a subjective judgement but this can be based on certain well founded economic principles. Coins are not made until the concept of coinage is understood: that is to say, they are created by an act of government for some public purpose. Ancient gold coins bought men and services, rewarded and confirmed loyalty, demonstrated power; strong rulers and states accumulated gold, weak ones paid it away. In brief, coins were not automotive; they were made for a purpose, fulfilled (however imperfectly) that purpose, and, once out of their issuers' hands, may have fulfilled other secondary purposes. One may think of the individual coin in the same light as a hypothetical gold £5 piece in 19th century Zululand—a country which offers curious analogies to the relationship between Celtic tribes and the Roman Empire.

Now at last to the question of 'what?' Like the Celts of Gaul we have one fixed point, the Gallic War. For us this means Caesar's invasions of 55–54 BC, so we begin our investigation by defining the coins certainly attributable to this period. Dr Scheers's work, fortunately, gives us our starting point. She has convincingly argued (1972) that the Belgic sinews for the Gallic War were what she calls 'uniface staters of the Ambiani' and we call Gallo-Belgic E (Fig 21). Of the seven classes into which Dr Scheers divides this coinage (1977: 334 series 24), only the first four are systematically found in Britain; in the course of their issue, the average weight falls steadily from *c* 6.30g to *c* 5.90g, and the gold fineness, at *c* 60% for classes 1–3, falls to *c* 50% in class 4. Her class 5 is never found in Britain, class 6 (Gallo-Belgic Xc1) (Fig 22) but rarely; gold fineness remains in the region of 50%, but there appears to be a significant increase in the proportion of copper to silver in the debasing alloy, and the weight is no more than 5.60g. Class 7 is a degraded issue, made entirely of bronze, and is, in Dr Scheers's view, the latest coinage of the independent Belgae. The entire coinage should begin not earlier than 58 BC and cease not later than 51 BC.

The distribution map (Fig 44) shows British find spots. The whole coinage is of continental Belgic origin, so what does this mean? We think at once of Caesar's remark (*BG* iv.20) that he understood that in almost all of the Gallic wars, help had been furnished from Britain to his enemies. I suggest that this help had to be bought, and was paid for between 58 and 55 BC in classes 1–4 of Gallo-Belgic E staters. The distribution shows, in general terms, the areas from which such help was obtained, and we are reminded that Caesar knew of two paramount tribes, the Trinovantes, *firmissima civitas*, and the unnamed people of Cassivellaunus. With Gallo-Belgic E should probably also be considered the finds of Gallo-Belgic C, Scheers's 'Ambianic staters with types on both sides' (Fig 23). British examples are all of her latest three classes (Scheers 1977, 268, series 9). It is noteworthy that coins of her classes 3 and 4 are in fact die-linked with early coins of the uniface series, and it is therefore likely that they are closely successive. I conclude that this great input of gold coin into south-eastern Britain took place in the four years preceding Caesar's in-

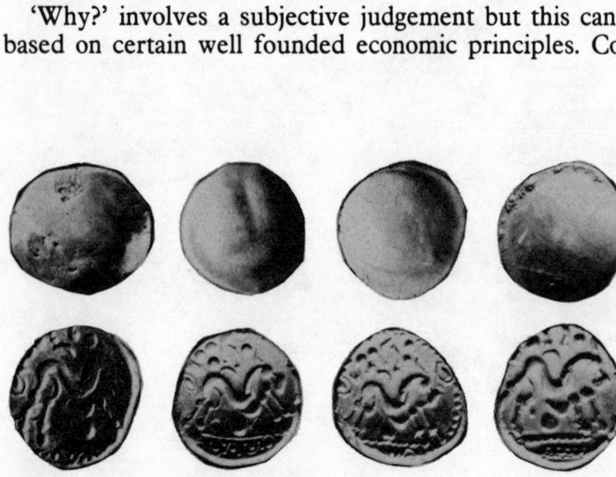

Fig 21 Gallo-Belgic E staters, classes I–IV

Fig 22 Gallo-Belgic E stater, class VI

Fig 23 Gallo-Belgic C staters, classes III–V

Fig 25 Two varieties of Gallo-Belgic Xc2 quarter stater

vasions. Gallo-Belgic C staters found in Britain have an average weight of *c* 6.45g and a gold fineness of 70%.

It is noteworthy that British A (Fig 24), the earliest British gold coinage, derives its typology from Gallo-Belgic C, but its weight and fineness from Gallo-Belgic E; it may have been provoked and made possible by the sudden availability of gold at a critical moment. I have suggested elsewhere (Kent 1978a) that the first issuer of gold coin in Britain was Cassivellaunus, and that early derivative coinages, soon petering out, are attributable to the Trinovantes (British E,F,G), Iceni (British J), and Coritani (British H,I). The problem of the British Atrebates has so far not been tackled. The south coast is the veritable land of the quarter stater, not the least numerous variety being Allen Xc2 (Fig 25), readily distinguishable by the letter ∧\ on the otherwise plain obverse. They are clearly related to Dr Scheers's class 6 of the Gallo-Belgic E staters, whose obverse is precisely the same. They differ in two important ways: first, provenance—quarter-staters are exclusively British, staters are mostly continental; secondly, composition—quarter staters have an average content of 56% gold, 15% silver, and 29% copper, staters contain 50% gold, 22% silver, and 28% copper. So the quarter-staters, though of appreciably finer gold, already show that shift from a silver-rich to a copper-rich alloy of all later British Celtic gold coin. This dominance of copper over silver occurs only in the very latest continental gold, such as the last issues of the Nervii (Scheers 1977, 394, series 29). The apparent abrupt shift from a Belgic to a British south-coast centre inevitably recalls the career of Commius of the Gallic Atrebates, who fled to Britain in 52 BC after the failure of the great revolt of that year. Caesar knew him to be a man 'of great authority' in Britain; just how great he was not to find out until it was too late. ∧\ for Atrebates rather than for Ambiani? This would certainly reconcile the British and Gallic find-spots and furnish another, if not particularly useful, fixed point in our chronology. Note that the Le Catillon hoard does not furnish a *terminus ante quem* of 51 BC for the Durotrigian silver coinage, as has been

suggested (Colbert de Beaulieu 1955). The concentration of hoards on Jersey and the miscellaneous character of the hoard from Rozel Bay seem rather to imply that that island became a place of refuge from Armorica and elsewhere in Gaul; the true *terminus ante quem* for these deposits is probably some twenty years later.

We have up to now been considering the origins of the minting of gold coin in Britain. Gallo-Belgic C staters are not by any means the earliest coins to be widely available here. This distinction is shared by two types, Dr Scheers's 'broad flan' issue of the Ambiani (Scheers 1977, 242, series 8) (Gallo-Belgic A, Fig 26), and the 'crossed lines' issue of the Caleti (*ibid*, 281, series 10) (Gallo-Belgic B, Fig 27). The distribution of the former (Fig 40) closely resembles that of Gallo-Belgic E (Fig 44); that of the latter is concentrated in the Home Counties around London (Fig 41). Their dates are quite uncertain; guesses have ranged from the mid 2nd century to the early 1st century BC (Kent 1978a, 313). It is certain that in Britain some of both types were available to be hoarded in and after *c* 60 BC, and although such pieces are generally much worn, I am reluctant to accept a really early date. If indeed the Belgae bought help against Caesar, there is no reason to think that this was the first time; at the risk of associating the coins with the one historical circumstance known to us, we might think of some episode in the doubtless spectacular career of Diviciacus of the Suessiones, in the early 1st century BC.

The distribution of Gallo-Belgic B is of particular interest. In its homeland, the Département of Seine-Maritime, this is a coinage of quarter-staters only. With a single exception, all recorded provenances of staters are British, and we seem to have a situation in which staters were struck 'for export only', perhaps implying that a single stater bought a specific commodity, and perhaps, too, that quarter-staters also had a particular function. The British distribution is remarkable in that it is unrelated to any later one. It seems to imply a centre just west of London (Kent 1978a, 319; 1978b, 53–8), and since no such centre seems to have been known to Caesar, it presumably no longer retained its importance in his day. The other evidence for such a centre is impressive. There is along this part of the Thames valley an important concentration of fine metalwork of the late Iron Age, and there are above all the Class I potin coins (Figs 27, 49). Individual specimens are widely scattered, but there is a great concentration of hoards along the north bank of the Thames from Gunnersbury to St James's Park. The pre-Caesarian date of the continental prototype is not in question, and, if the exotic

Fig 24 British A staters, classes I & II

Fig 26 Gallo-Belgic A stater

Fig 27 Gallo-Belgic B stater

Fig 28 British potin, class I

material from Snettisham is really part of a single complex, then we should have the association of potins with Gallo-Belgic A and C gold, and a date not much before Caesar's invasion of Britain. The concentration of so high a proportion of the potin coins into hoards in a very restricted area suggests a brief existence terminated by an emergency. Some important move not long before 55 BC in the expansion of Cassivellaunus's realm might provide a suitable occasion, with the destruction of 'proto-London' and its incipient monetary economy. Two major finds suggest the flight of moneyed people at this time—Snettisham, Norfolk (Gallo-Belgic A + C + ? potin Class I); Carn Brea, Cornwall (Gallo-Belgic A + B).

The development of British coinage after the Gallic War is a long, complex, and often obscure story that has no part in this paper. My aim here is to suggest that we reject the concept of coinage in Britain linked to invasions or migrations of peoples, and interpret it as the outcome of the interaction of related political and economic events. Some old favourites may face an uncertain future. The Catuvellauni, for example, collapse back into the obscurity accorded them by the ancient sources, while Cassivellaunus seems to have affinities with Wessex rather than north of the Thames. And the Trinovantes emerge as the real beneficiaries of Caesar's invasions—as indeed we might have guessed all along!

Bibliography

Burgon, T, 1839 *Numis Chron*, 36

Colbert de Beaulieu, J–B, 1955 Armorican hoards in the Channel Islands, *Proc Prehist Soc*, **21**, 210

Kent, J P C, 1978a The origins and development of Celtic gold coinage in Britain, *Actes du Congrès International d'Archéologie: Rouen, 3, 4, 5 juillet 1975*, 313–24

Kent, J P C, 1978b The London area in the Late Iron Age: an interpretation of the earliest coins, *Collectanea Londiniensia: studies presented to Ralph Merrifield*, 53–8

Nash, D, 1975 The chronology of Celtic coinage in Gaul: the Arvernian 'hegemony' reconsidered, *Numis Chron*, **15**, 7 ser, 204–188

Scheers, S, 1972 Coinage and currency of the Belgic tribes during the Gallic War, *Brit Numis J*, 1–6

Scheers, S, 1977 *Traité de numismatique celtique* **II:** *La Gaule Belgique*

Lost and found: the archaeology of find-spots of Celtic coins *Warwick Rodwell*

While the distribution map is one of the most useful tools employed by the archaeologist to express spatial relationships, it is nevertheless frequently called into question. Satisfactory substitutes, however, seem seldom to be forthcoming. No one would dispute that there are demonstrable biases which affect most kinds of distribution map, but coin distributions are amongst those which have tacitly been assumed reasonably secure. The basis for this assumption has been the belief that the vast majority of finds of Celtic coins in Britain, and especially gold and silver coins, have been of a random and casual nature. Do distribution maps of coin finds really reflect the patterns of ancient coin losses, let alone the patterns of usage?

The sociology of archaeological finds-reporting has been studied by the writer over the last decade or so, with particular reference to Essex, and the function of this paper is to draw attention to factors which are of considerable importance to the archaeologist in understanding the processes whereby casual finds of coins enter Sites and Monuments Records. The paper is in two parts: in the first I have assembled the evidence for Celtic coin losses in Essex, taking a critical look at what sort of coins have been found, in which locations, under what circumstances, and by whom. This is concluded by a brief consideration of the implications for the archaeologist when find-patterns are equated with loss-patterns. In the second part of the paper I shall outline some of the general factors which can be demonstrated or surmised to have had an effect on the loss, recovery, and reporting of Celtic coins in Britain.

I Celtic coin-finds in Essex: an analysis

It has been observed by Dr John Collis that finds of coins in different metals do not support similar distribution patterns, and that while gold coins are found in considerable numbers in the countryside, bronze coinage is more plentiful in oppida and major settlements (Collis 1971; 1974). He went on to suggest that this may be a result of these coinages having had different functions in the Iron Age, and being used by different social groups. In an appendix to a paper which discussed late Iron Age settlement in south-eastern Britain, I ventured an alternative interpretation, suggesting that coin distributions, as we now see and use them, do not reflect so much the original patterns of circulation and loss as the patterns of modern collection and identification (Rodwell 1976a, 313–16). That contention is worthy of consideration in greater detail, since its implications for the value of distribution maps are considerable. A sample area has been chosen for detailed study, corresponding to the historic county of Essex.

No better area than Essex could have been chosen, since it lies near the centre of the distribution of Celtic coins in south-eastern Britain, where all coin metals and a very wide range of issues are known to have circulated. Essex has been an almost totally agricultural landscape for upwards of 200 years, and there have thus been equal chances for the discovery of coins throughout the whole county. Furthermore, the topography of the county is such that no parts are inaccessible or uninhabitable, save a relatively minute area of coastal marshland: there the present land surfaces are of post Iron Age date. Finally, it has become clear from intensive studies over the last decade or so that the landscape was densely settled from early prehistoric times, and that by the late Iron Age the widespread forest cover which is so often wished upon the area by undiscerning writers

had been drastically reduced and brought under control. There is thus no plausible reason related to natural topography or basic settlement history why any specific areas in the county should be devoid of later Iron Age settlement or coinage. If the average density of Iron Age settlements were as low as two per parish, that would make about 850 sites in the county; in those areas where adequate field survey has taken place it is not uncommon to find three or four Iron Age sites in a parish. The potential number of Celtic coins lost in the county must run into many tens of thousands, at least.

Although I have looked into and recorded as far as possible the circumstances relating to the discovery of every Celtic coin from the county, it is clearly impossible to present the evidence in full, and it has therefore to be rationalized under convenient headings.

The topography of find-spots

There are just over one thousand recorded finds of Celtic coins from Essex (Fig 29), exclusive of the hoards from Clacton, Marks Tey, Colchester, and Epping Forest. These hoards together add at least another 245 coins to the total. Of the one thousand, about 351 have been found at Harlow and 278 at Camulodunum-Colchester. For present purposes Camulodunum and Colchester are considered as one site, and so, too, are Harlow temple and town. When these two exceptionally prolific sites are set aside, there remains a total of about 375 coins collected from between 54 and 75 locations. No greater precision is possible in determining the number of find-spots, since there are at least a dozen instances where coins have been recorded on several separate occasions in a given parish, and there is now no way of telling how many individual archaeological sites were involved.

I have taken the gross distribution of find-spots of Celtic coins in Essex and plotted these against various background factors, with the following results. First, it may be noted that there is no correlation between find-spots and the physical topography of the landscape (Fig 29): no coins seem to have been found above the 250ft contour or on the marshes, but between those two extremes there is no discernible pattern. Nor is there any meaningful relationship to river valleys: concentrations can be seen in the lower reaches of the Lea, close to London, and along the upper reaches of the Pant, beyond Braintree, but neither on topographical nor archaeological grounds is there any cause to differentiate between these and other river valleys in the county.

When coins are plotted against drift geology, an equally indecisive result is obtained (Fig 30). Here it may be seen that about half the find-spots fall on the lighter soils (loams and gravels), or on their interfaces with heavier lands, but the remainder fall on the Boulder Clay and London Clay. Even more equivocal are the results obtained from plotting find-spots against known sites of the Iron Age and Roman periods: in some parts of the county there are numerous coin finds from areas where dense settlement is known (eg around Southend-on-Sea), but elsewhere the coins are lacking although the settlement evidence is plentiful (eg the Grays–Thurrock area, on the Thames, and the Tendring peninsula east of Colchester).

If, then, the coin distribution is not closely related to natural features or ancient settlements, it seems inescapable that modern factors must dominate the pattern. I have

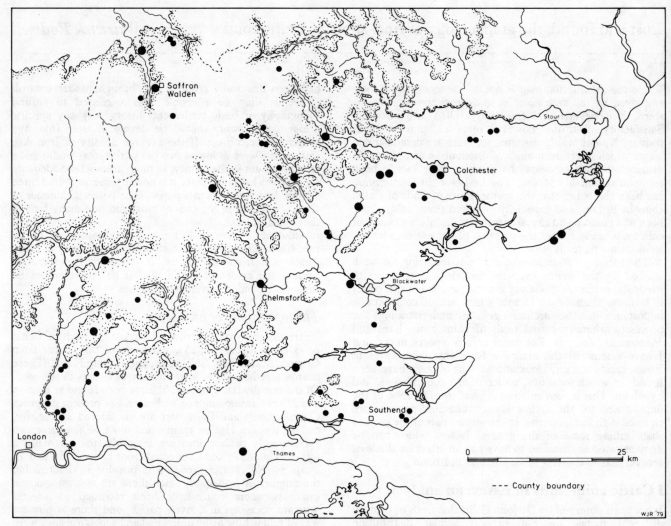

Fig 29 Overall distribution of find-spots of Celtic coins from Essex, in relation to topography; the 200ft contour is shown

produced elsewhere a map which illustrates, admittedly in very simple terms, the various levels of archaeological recording in Essex, based on fieldwork and excavation over the last century or so (Rodwell 1976b, fig 2). The correlation between that map and the overall coin distribution in Essex is impressive, and although it is frequently said, in a light-hearted manner, that distribution maps reflect no more than the pattern of archaeologists on the ground, this has seldom been tested as a serious hypothesis. On Fig 31 the principal agencies through which Celtic coins have been recorded (along with many other classes of artefact) are indicated in their respective areas:

Excavations   All the large and medium-sized collections are derived from excavations and informed searches of excavated sites.

London-based interests   Most of the coins from south-west Essex can be traced back to the activities of London-based collectors and antiquaries.

Southend area   Most of the coins found in south-east Essex have come to light during the development of the area around Southend-on-Sea during the last fifty years. These have mainly been recorded at Southend Museum.

Cambridge-based interests   The cluster of finds from north-west Essex relates to the active interests of two or three antiquaries; most notable here was

Lord Braybrooke and his work in the vicinity of Great Chesterford.

Colchester-based interests   The recording of coin finds from the Colchester area and, to a lesser extent, from north-east Essex has largely been due to the interests of a handful of well-known antiquaries (William Wire, George Joslin, Rev J H Pollexfen, and Philip and Henry Laver) and, more recently, careful recording by the late M R Hull.

Other local antiquaries   Elsewhere in Essex there have been neither strong nor long-lived antiquarian traditions which could be considered alongside Colchester, Cambridge, and London. From time to time, however, local clergy and gentry have formed small collections or handed down records of discoveries which were brought to their attention. Several of the men in question lived in the small market towns of central Essex, and it is thus no mere coincidence that Chelmsford, Maldon, Braintree, and Halstead are each accredited with several finds of Celtic coins, mainly of gold.

Thus the mechanics of recording finds of Celtic coins can be studied, understood, and put into perspective. When this has been done it may readily be seen how and why gross coin distributions form the patterns which are familiar to us through maps.

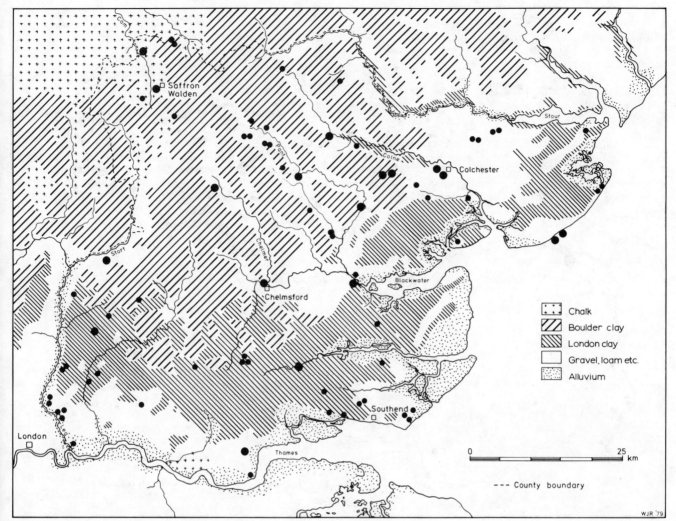

Fig 30 Overall distribution of find-spots of Celtic coins from Essex, in relation to drift geology

Distribution of coins by metal type

Gold   There have been upwards of 96 single finds of gold coins in Essex, of which 24 have come from Colchester, 11 from Harlow, and 61 from elsewhere. If the hoards from Clacton, Marks Tey, Colchester, and Epping Forest are added, the total rises to 210, at least (contemporary forgeries are not included in these figures). The gross distribution of gold coins (Fig 32) is identical to the general distribution of all Celtic coins from Essex (Fig 29), and since there are many more find-spots of gold than any other metal, it is essentially gold which has determined the distribution pattern. The exact number of find-spots cannot be determined, for reasons given earlier (above, p 43), but it must be at least fifty. Gold coins have only been recovered from two excavations—Harlow temple and Wickford—but informed searching, especially at Colchester, must have yielded a few from well known sites.

Silver   In contrast to gold, only 35 Celtic silver coins have been reported from Essex; these have all come from seven sites, four of which have been excavated (Fig 33). Of the total, 24 coins are from Colchester-Camulodunum and six from Harlow, leaving only five from the remainder of the county. It is interesting to observe that while Colchester and Harlow have yielded significant numbers of both gold and silver coins, in terms of recorded finds from other sites

the gold outnumbers the silver by ten to one (contemporary forgeries are not included in these figures, nor are the fifteen silver coins from the mixed hoard at Colchester).

Bronze   Upwards of 590 bronze coins have been recorded, of which 550 have been found at Colchester and Harlow; the remainder are drawn from fourteen sites (Fig 34). Of the forty or so coins in question, 32 have been derived from excavations at Wickford, Kelvedon, Billericay, Mucking, Chelmsford, Stanway, and Gestingthorpe, leaving only eight coins as casual finds from six separate sites. At least two of those were derived from informed searches.

Potin   Twenty-six potin coins have been recorded from eleven find-spots in Essex (Fig 35); almost half the total have been found in excavations at Wickford and Kelvedon, while others have come from excavations at Great Chesterford, Heybridge, Mucking, Gestingthorpe, Witham, and Billericay. This leaves only three casual finds from the county, one of which is dubious. It is a remarkable fact that not a single potin coin has been recorded at Harlow or Colchester (but see Rodwell 1976a, 207), although there are three unprovenanced coins in the Pollexfen collection in Colchester Museum, which are presumably derived from the area.

The implications to be drawn from these figures are so overwhelmingly clear as to need little comment: coins of all

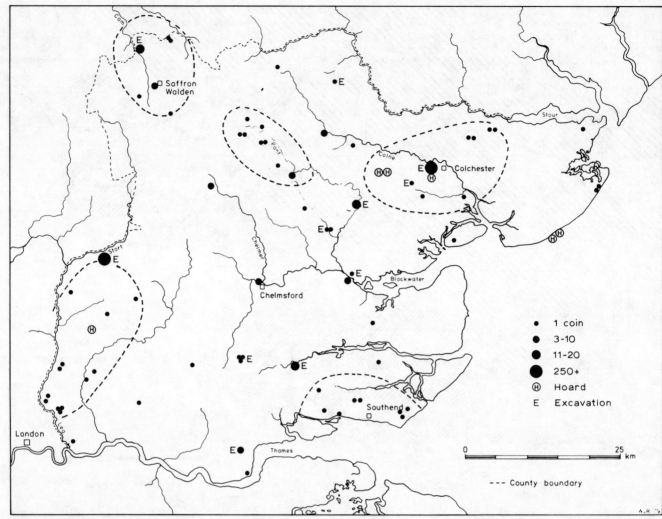

Fig 31 Map to illustrate factors known to have influenced the collection and recording of Celtic coins in Essex. The dotted lines define areas where particular collecting and recording interests are known

metals can be found by excavation or informed search on sites of the later Iron Age in all parts of the county. Over the past two centuries finds of gold coins have attracted the attention of antiquaries only in those areas where an established interest was known to exist. Regardless of the numbers of silver, bronze, and potin coins which have actually been found in uncontrolled circumstances, the total of recorded specimens is almost negligible: the reporting of casual finds of gold coins is ten times more frequent than that for other metals.

Composition of site coin lists

It has been observed elsewhere (Rodwell 1976a, 313–16) that coin lists from unexcavated sites tend to be heavily weighted in favour of precious metals, while those from extensively excavated sites show a preponderance of bronze. When percentage calculations are based solely upon material recovered from excavations, a small amount of silver is usually present, but seldom any gold. As we have observed, gold coins have only been derived from two excavations in Essex, although plated forgeries of gold coins have turned up on most excavations which have yielded Celtic coins.

In the second part of this paper we will be considering the possible reasons why gold coins seemingly fail to appear on excavations, but first we will examine some coin lists

from sites in Essex in detail. Five sites have yielded sufficient numbers of coins to attempt meaningful comparison. There are two prolific sites, Colchester-Camulodunum and Harlow (temple and town), and three smaller sites, Great Chesterford, Kelvedon, and Wickford. These are well spaced out around the county, and any local bias which might affect one could hardly affect the others. For comparison, another site of the smaller category, Baldock (Herts), is also included. The numbers of coins found in each metal and their percentages in relation to the site total, of both excavated and chance finds, are given in Table I and the results are summarized in a bar chart (Fig 36).

It is meaningless to read too much into individual figures and percentages, when the actual number of coins being considered is not great. The general trends are, however, clear: all sites are likely to yield both British and Gaulish coins of all metals (within the relevant geographical and chronological constraints of the various types). Potin is the least common, followed next by silver, and then by gold. On the information available for study it is not possible to suggest that there are any significant differences between the proportions of metals present on any two sites. Thus in terms of numbers of coins, those sites which have yielded numerous bronzes have also yielded relatively high numbers of gold and silver issues. Furthermore, the greater the

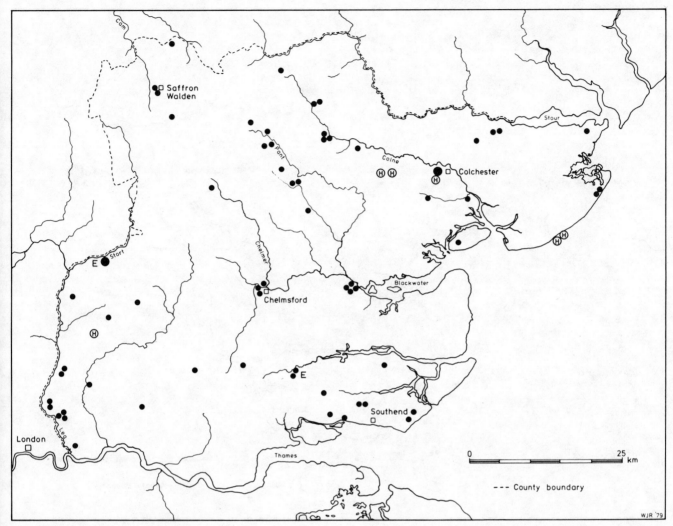

Fig 32 Distribution of Celtic gold coins in Essex

number of coins in precious metals, the greater, too, are the number of contemporary forgeries, which strongly suggests that genuine coins and forgeries circulated side by side and without any functional differences (Rodwell 1976a, 314). The generally mixed nature of coins in use in an *oppidum* is perhaps indicated by the Colchester hoard, which contained 25 gold, 15 silver, and 20 bronze issues (Allen 1960, 292).

II Discovery and recording of coins: some problems

There are many factors which affect the processes inherent in the loss, rediscovery, and recording of coins; some are obvious and will not be dwelt upon.

Original pattern of loss

It is not our intention here to consider patterns of minting or circulation, or forms of use of Celtic coinages, although these all obviously condition the possible loss patterns. Clearly, the more coins there are in use in a given area, and the more times they change hands, the greater will be the number of losses; and coins of low value are always lost more freely than those of high value. In general terms it may be said that if it were possible to construct a contour map of original coin losses it would be as intricate as a piece of highland topography: we should not expect uniformity.

Ancient disturbances to the ground

Ancient disturbances can have two opposing effects. First, they can diminish the coin yield from a site: the more the ground is disturbed, the more the coins will tend to come to the surface, where they can decay or be picked up (as money *per se*, as curiosities, or as scrap metal: here it may be noted that non-ferrous metals have always had a sufficient scrap value to make their collection worthwhile, even in quite small quantities). On a site where there has been long occupation and much disturbance of the ground, there will have been a continual process of diminution in its coin content. On the other hand, a considerable number of coins, particularly those of gold and silver, which have been found on archaeological sites are equally as likely to be the result of dispersed hoards as they are to be derived from casual losses. There is ample evidence to show that coins, mainly other than bronze, were hoarded in large numbers in the Iron Age. Obviously, we have only recovered in modern times a small proportion of those hoards which were buried in the ground and have remained intact. Building works and agriculture, from the Roman period onwards, will have broken up and scattered a far greater number of hoards. There must, for example, be many instances which cannot now be verified where a hoard was disturbed in antiquity and many of the coins perhaps recovered from the ground, leaving just a few scattered in the soil, which have

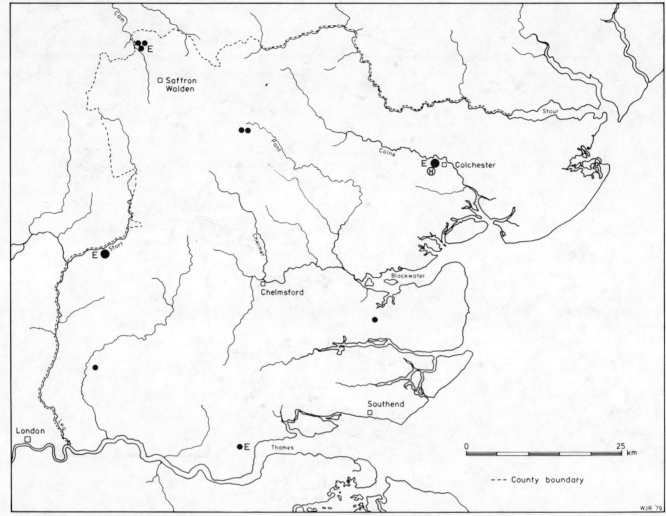

Fig 33 Distribution of Celtic silver coins in Essex

subsequently turned up as 'casual' finds. The burial of coin hoards in the ground is only one form of concealment: just as many were probably hidden under wooden floors, in walls, roofs, trees, and so on. None of these can now be recovered as hoards *per se*, but there can be no denying that their dispersal through the processes of natural decay and disaster must be responsible for a certain proportion of site finds and modern casual finds.

In summary, the implications of ancient disturbances to the ground are: first, that coins of all denominations will have been retrieved, and secondly, that the introduction of loose coins into the soil after the Iron Age will, on account of hoarding practices, be weighted almost entirely in favour of gold and silver.

Modern disturbances to the ground

Here the factors affecting recovery are massively variable. First, ground which has been farmed for centuries will have had its coin yield depleted steadily by generations of agricultural workers. Gold and silver coins, being more easily recognizable, will have been recovered in far greater numbers than bronze. Not only will the latter have been missed, but thousands must also have decayed through exposure and soil action. Advances in agriculture over the past fifty years will not only have caused a vast increase in the numbers of coins brought to the surface, but at the same

time, by reducing the need for manual labour, will have drastically diminished the chances of their early recovery.

Character and honesty of finders

Every year, some hundreds of Celtic coins change hands through the major London salerooms, and these must only represent the tip of the iceberg. It is probably no exaggeration to suggest that a thousand or more Celtic coins are unearthed each year in Britain: doubtless many are never recognized for what they are, and the number which actually gets recorded properly is very low indeed.

Until the early part of this century, the agricultural worker who found a coin could either conceal it indefinitely or hand it over to the landowner, who might in due course show it to a museum or an antiquary of his acquaintance. The great majority of records relating to the finding of Celtic coins in Britain before *c* 1920 show this process in action. Up to that time the average labourer could not easily dispose of coins for cash, without raising suspicions: the best hope of gaining a reward for one's find was through honesty.

The labourer who lived in or close to a town of some size was in a different position: he could sell coins to jewellers, pawnbrokers, and people whom he might meet in public houses, without too many questions being asked or the likelihood of the landowner finding out. Thus one can point

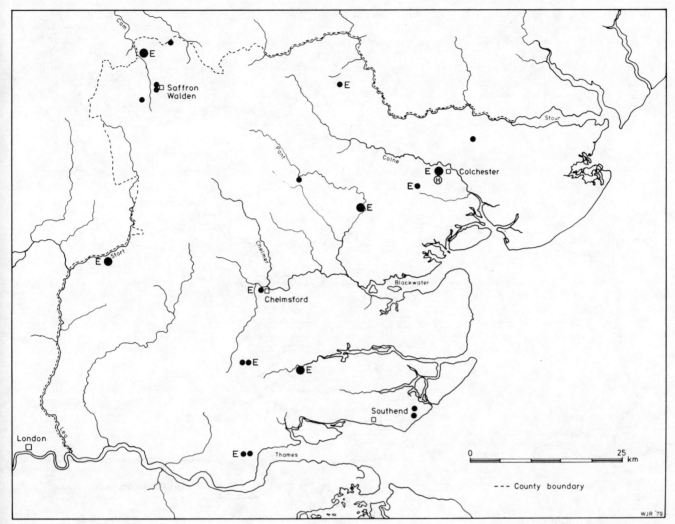

Fig 34 Distribution of Celtic bronze coins in Essex

to many records of coins bearing deliberately vague provenances, such as 'found near Colchester' or 'bought in Colchester'. Hence in the 19th century men such as William Wire—jeweller, pawnbroker, and antiquary in Colchester —managed to acquire many fine specimens of Celtic coins with few or no details of provenances. Wire was one of the more conscientious antiquaries of his day, whose diaries constitute an invaluable archaeological record; nevertheless, from a professional point of view he clearly knew when it was better not to ask questions about the exact provenance and ownership of the antiquities that were brought to him.

Although the site of Camulodunum must have been yielding a constant stream of Celtic coins for centuries, it can be no coincidence that very few indeed are provenanced to that site before the excavations of the 1930s. Although incapable of proof, it is very likely that many of the gold staters and half-staters in the British Museum and Colchester Museum which are known to have come from the Colchester area, or from collectors living there, were in fact from Camulodunum.

In contrast to this assertion is the curious fact that although gold-plated and silver coins were found during the excavations at Sheepen in 1930–9, alongside a large number of bronze coins, not a single gold coin features on the list (Hawkes & Hull 1947, 133–42). This apparent lack of excavated gold at Camulodunum has been remarked upon by various writers (eg Collis 1974), and I have previously

drawn attention to the conflicting evidence (Rodwell 1976, 313–16). To suggest that gold coins might have been found at Sheepen but not handed in to the excavation supervisors will doubtless be considered outrageous by some, and a lame excuse by others, but I nevertheless put it forward as a possibility.

Interests of museums and archaeologists

It is an observable fact that a disproportionately high number of gold and silver coins are reported to museums; bronze coins (apart from large Roman issues) are not only more difficult to observe in the ground, but they also attract less curiosity as to value. Equally, it is an observable fact that not only do coins constitute a high proportion of the recorded archaeological finds from remote rural areas, but they are also mainly of precious metals. In general, the finders of gold and silver coins expend more effort on getting them identified than the finders of bronze. This has important implications for the Iron Age, since it is likely to be the root cause of the apparent dominance of gold coinage in rural areas.

The truth of this observation is amply borne out by reference to the Roman period; for Essex I have made a comparable study. There is a thin scatter of Roman gold coins recorded across Essex; they number at least twenty and most were recorded under conditions directly

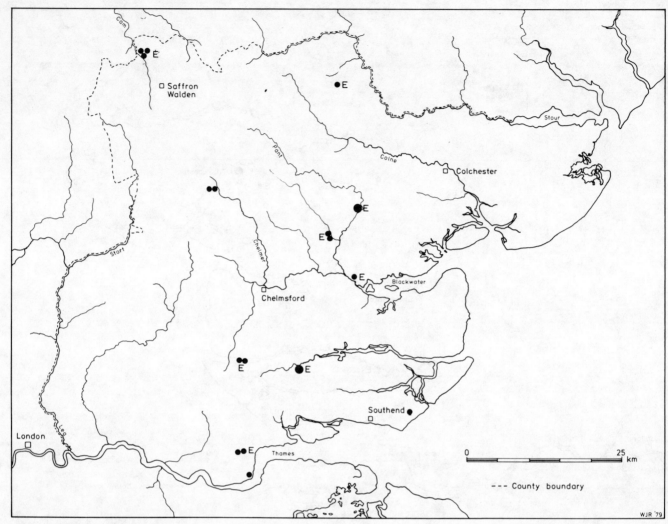

Fig 35 Distribution of potin coins in Essex

comparable to those obtaining for the Celtic gold coins. I am not aware that a single Roman example has been found in a controlled excavation. The argument can be taken a stage further by noting that more gold solidi of Honorius and Arcadius have been reported as casual finds than have bronze coins of the same emperors; yet when excavating late Roman sites it is only the bronze coins which seem to turn up. In general, the records of casual finds of Roman coins from Essex, before the era of metal-detector prospection, were heavily weighted in favour of the large bronze issues of the early and middle Empire and gold issues. Small, late Roman bronze coins, which are about the same size as their Celtic counterparts, have proved to be far more numerous on excavated sites than the larger and earlier issues. The acknowledged interest or physical presence of an antiquary in a country town or village has often, in the past, been responsible for the finding and recording of Celtic bronze coins, in circumstances where they would otherwise have been overlooked. In Braintree the Rev J W Kenworthy fulfilled such a role at the beginning of this century. But nowhere is the process more clearly demonstrated than at Braughing, where the active interest of Sir John Evans was directly responsible for the mid 19th century records of bronze coin finds at this site.

In recent years circumstances have changed considerably with the blight of metal detectors and the rapid rise in the cash value of coins. There is a massive distrust of museums in all levels of society (although for different reasons) and less and less material is being reported, relative to the amount which is being unearthed. Furthermore, it is interesting to note that many finds are not being reported at the nearest museum, but are being shown at museums many miles from their find-spots. This inevitably has an adverse effect on the recording of such finds and their publication.

Through a long and discreet association with collectors, dealers, and salerooms, the late D F Allen was able to record some thousands of Celtic coins—with and without specific provenances—many of which would otherwise have escaped the archaeological record altogether. Since his death the volume of new information being recorded each year has fallen dramatically.

In summary, we may say that from the mid 19th to the mid 20th century there was a recognizable pattern in the discovery and recording of Celtic coins. There were local variations within this pattern, which resulted in particular peaks of recording. However, changes in attitudes and values, especially over the last decade, have totally destroyed earlier patterns, and the recording of Celtic coins, with any hope of achieving even a modest level of efficiency, has now become an unattainable goal. Finally, coin finds from excavations, which are usually assumed to be free from biases towards certain metals and denominations, must be viewed more realistically and due

Table 1   Percentages of coins from five selected sites, according to metal, authenticity, and origin
(Actual numbers of coins given in parenthesis)

	AV	AV plated	AR British	AR plated	AR Gaulish	AE British	AE Gaulish	Potin British	Potin Gaulish
Camulodunum-Colchester	8.63	2.88	8.27	0.72	0.36	77.34	1.80	0	0
(278 coins)	(24)	(8)	(23)	(2)	(1)	(215)	(5)	(0)	(0)
Harlow temple and town	3.13	1.14	1.71	0	0	94.02	0	0	0
(351 coins)	(11)	(4)	(6)	(0)	(0)	(330)	(0)	(0)	(0)
Great Chesterford, Essex	5.26	0	10.53	0	5.26	63.16	0	10.53	5.26
(19 coins)	(1)	(0)	(2)	(0)	(1)	(12)	(0)	(2)	(1)
Kelvedon, Essex	0	7.14	0	0	0	42.86	0	42.86	7.14
(14 coins)	(0)	(1)	(0)	(0)	(0)	(6)	(0)	(6)	(1)
Wickford, Essex	12.50	12.50	0	0	0	43.75	6.25	25.00	0
(16 coins)	(2)	(2)	(0)	(0)	(0)	(7)	(1)	(4)	(0)
Baldock, Herts	3.92	1.96	3.92	0	0	78.43	1.96	9.80	0
(51 coins)	(2)	(1)	(2)	(0)	(0)	(40)	(1)	(5)	(0)
Totals (728)	(39)	(16)	(33)	(2)	(2)	(610)	(7)	(17)	(2)
Average percentages	5.57	4.27	4.07	0.12	0.94	66.60	1.67	14.70	2.07
Combined averages	9.84		5.13			68.27		16.76	

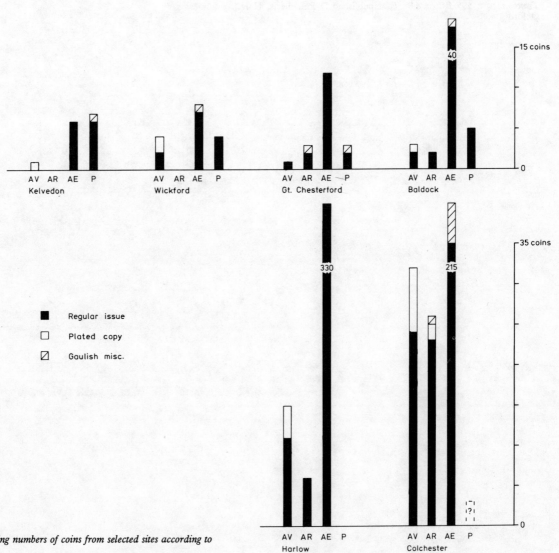

Fig 36 Bar chart showing numbers of coins from selected sites according to metal

allowance made for human failings which are known to exist but which cannot, unfortunately, be measured with precision. Hence we must accept distribution maps as providing only the coarsest general overview of coin circulation and loss patterns. Clusters and voids within these distribution patterns, particularly for metals other than gold, must be discounted as meaningless unless they can be shown to be other than accidents of antiquarianism and excavation.

Time and again one may point to the apparent 'split' distributions of certain coin issues in northern Essex and Hertfordshire (eg Rodwell 1976a, figs 20, 29, 32): the explanation for these does not lie in obscure social or economic structures in the Iron Age, but simply in the collecting and excavating habits of antiquaries and archaeologists.

Bibliography

Allen, D F, 1960 The origins of coinage in Britain: a reappraisal, in Frere, S S (ed), *Problems of the Iron Age in southern Britain*, 97–308

Collis, J R, 1971 Functional and theoretical interpretations of British coinage, *World Archaeol*, 3, 71–84

Collis, J R, 1974 'A functional approach to pre-Roman coinage', in Casey, P J, & Reece, R M (eds), *Coins and the archaeologist* 1–11

Hawkes, C F C & Hull, M R, 1947 *Camulodunum*

Rodwell, W J, 1976a 'Coinage, oppida and the rise of Belgic power in south-eastern Britain', in Cunliffe, B W & Rowley, R T (eds), *Oppida: The beginnings of urbanisation in barbarian Europe*, 181–367

Rodwell, W J, 1976b *Settlement and economy in the territory of the Trinovantes, c 500 BC to AD 50*, unpublished D Phil thesis, Univ Oxford

Coinage, oppida, and the rise of Belgic power: a reply *John Collis*

The conflicts of the 1960s between advocates of the 'new archaeology' and adherents to the traditional 'historical paradigm' have found a reflection in pre-Roman numismatics in the 1970s. The traditional school epitomized in the writings of the late Derek Allen has been championed primarily by Harding (1974) and Rodwell (1976), while the 'newmismatic' school has been voiced in a series of papers by Haselgrove, Hodder, and myself. Rodwell's recent attacks, primarily on my early papers (1971a, 1971b, 1974a), however, require some generalized reply as it seems to me that the lessons that many of us learnt in the 1960s are going to be forgotten in the 1980s, to the detriment of future research. I have added an appendix to reply to some more specific criticisms.

Our differences, however, are much more fundamental than mere facts. It could be construed as a simple conflict between 'historical' and 'socio-economic' interpretations of the coinage, or alternatively between the 'formalist' school of economics which interprets ancient economies in terms of the 19th century market economy (supply and demand, etc), as against the 'substantivist' school of Polanyi (1957) and Sahlins (1972), which envisages an economy 'embedded' in social relationships, resulting in very 'uneconomic' patterns appearing. Rodwell in his advocacy of market exchange mechanisms might be said to belong to the 'formalists'; I would certainly place myself among the 'substantivists'. But basically I think our differences lie in the conflict between 'inductive' and 'deductive' thinking—the former looks at a body of data and attempts to interpret it, the latter constructs hypothetical models and tests them against the data to see which fits best. It is the conflict between 'historical particularism', and model building to find more generally applicable interpretations.

The historical paradigm

The main aim of those who advocate an historical approach is the recognition of historical events in the archaeological record. Thus each set of data is unique, and has its own unique historical interpretation, hence the term 'historical particularism'. In the case of pre-Roman British coinage the aim is either to define areas of invasions by looking at the distribution of certain types of gold coins, or to delimit areas of political power. The main historical events are the Belgic invasion and Caesar's raids of 55 and 54 BC. There are, however, a number of tacit assumptions behind this approach, such as that coinage was produced by defined tribal groups, that the distribution reflects political or ethnic rather than social or economic factors, or that connexions across the English Channel did not exist in the period immediately before the introduction of coinage. It is worth noting also that there is a tacit selection of data: Gallo-Belgic coins reflect invasion, Armorican and potin coins do not. The spread of coin using throughout the rest of Europe is by adoption, but it is by invasion in Britain—so what makes Britain so different?

Another problem is the interpretation of the distribution maps themselves. What do odd outliers to the main distribution of coins mean, and how does one define an outlier? A glance through the maps in Rodwell's 1976 article shows they mean different things at different times. Here the bias in the collection and reporting of coins is at its most damaging (see below). But perhaps the most pertinent sentence concerning the invasionist approach is Rodwell's

statement on Owslebury, which he refers to as 'lying beyond the Belgic area' (Rodwell 1976, 297). Owslebury is 8 km south-east of Winchester, the Roman *Venta Belgarum*, but nowhere on his maps of 'Belgic' material does central Hampshire appear. On one of the few occasions when we can 'test' his archaeological assumptions with epigraphic data, they are found wanting. Because of its eclectic use of the data, and because of its untestability, I can only describe the historical approach as applied to the Iron Age as largely a pointless exercise.

My aims

My questions are basically very simple:
1 Who produced coins?
2 What were they produced for?
3 Who used them?
4 What did they use them for?

We can start off with the assumption that a society which only possessed high-value gold coins was not using them for the same functions as in our own society, and this principle can be extended to silver, potin, and bronze coins. That the primary intention behind producing coins is not necessarily that of the secondary usage can be demonstrated by an Athenian example: the obol was produced to pay individuals for state services such as military or jury service, but it was subsequently used for exchange, which quickly developed into an impersonal market-based exchange system. Whatever bronze coins were used for, it was rare, if not unknown, for a state to produce them specifically for retail exchange until the last couple of hundred years.

We can get some idea of the circumstances of production from the coins themselves (mint marks, etc), and from the debris of production—in the case of Iron Age coins the so-called coin moulds and, less usefully, unstruck flans and dies. We can see what sorts of sites these turn up on, and where on the site. In the past there has been an assumption that coin minting was confined to major sites, though I have postulated on purely hypothetical grounds that this need not be so in the Iron Age, and that production could take place on relatively minor sites (Collis 1971a). Though this idea has been strongly criticized (Wainwright & Spratling 1973; Megaw et al, 1973; Rodwell 1976, 282), recent finds have confirmed my conjecture, notably the evidence for gold and silver coin production at the small industrial village of Aulnat, Clermont Ferrand (Collis 1980). Of the forty or so sites which have produced fragments of 'moulds' (not all definite) only about fifteen or sixteen are certainly major defended oppida (Tournaire et al, in preparation), which suggests that production was by no means centralized on the major sites, though that is not to deny that it was not highly centralized in some cases—for instance in the kingdom of Cunobelin in the 1st century AD. However, the equation 'coin mould means major settlement' no longer holds, an important point in considering the status of 'unknown' sites such as Winchester (see Appendix, note 1). I still consider my theoretical discussion of control of minting a basic starting point for future work (Collis 1971a).

We can also observe the context of our coin finds. What sorts of site do they come from—urban, religious, high-class or low-class farms—and what was their context on major sites—high-status areas, trading areas, streets, or industrial zones? Is there evidence that different metal types turn up in different contexts, ie that bronze and gold for instance had different social and economic functions and, if so, what does it mean in terms of exchange systems? We are here dealing with a whole range of variables, such as distance to market, regularity of visit, social structure of the society, social status of the individuals trading, all of which could affect the pattern of coin using, as we can clearly see if we for instance compare medieval England with colonial post-medieval America, both of them with a partial development of coin using.

Sampling bias

Rodwell's main attack on my approach has now concentrated on the problem of sampling. The bias in the recorded finds is a matter that has long been recognized, and I have tried to elaborate precisely what sorts of biases occur at what stage (Haselgrove & Collis, below, pp 57–61; Collis 1974b) and I would advocate that my hypotheses based mainly on chance finds should be tested against the archaeologically excavated material as it becomes available. The problem of sampling bias is, however, much more damaging for Rodwell's historical approach, dealing as it does with unique historical interpretations of the data, and minor gaps in the material are of more consequence to him than to me, as he relies on the total distribution for his interpretations. My hypotheses, though they may be *suggested* by the total data, are in fact generally *testable* from individual sites and excavations, as for instance my suggestion that gold coins are primarily a phenomenon of the countryside, and bronze coins of the oppida.

However, I am sceptical that the situation is as bad as Rodwell suggests. New finds of coins tend to come from areas where old finds would lead us to expect them: eg coins of Cunobelin are not turning up in Cornwall or Scotland! His claims that finds from non-urban sites in Essex disprove my approach is hardly so: I may have painted a picture too strong in terms of black and white, but I remain sceptical that bronze coins were circulating freely on all sites as they were, say, in the 3rd century AD. His suggestion that the lack of gold coins from Colchester excavations is due to pilfering by the excavators makes me wonder if volunteers are more honest than rural sites: the farming site at Owslebury has produced a gold stater and the small village at Aulnat no fewer than two gold coins. Had Colchester produced numerous gold coins it would rather need to be explained why it was so different from all other oppida in central and western Europe.

Conclusions

In my articles I have attempted to act as devil's advocate in questioning many of the assumptions that have been tacitly made in the past, for instance that coinage was used in the same way as in our own society; that coin production was necessarily under centralized control; that coin production was a phenomenon confined to major settlements; that exchange systems even in coin-using societies operated through an open-market system. Nowhere have I 'assumed what I set out to prove' (Rodwell 1976, 280), but I have put forward attitudes of mind which do not negate other attitudes but do provide a different framework for thought. I have tried to test my hypotheses, I have admitted as with the potin coinage, where they are inconclusive, and equally I have no objection to people proving my hypotheses false. This is part of the process of testing, but it can only be done by dispassionate proof.

This debate is not only relevant to pre-Roman coinage, but also raises the whole question of where we are going with numismatic studies, for there seems to be a danger that we are going to slip back into the bad old ways in which opinion ruled. I believe passionately in the construction of

questions and models that can be *tested*, and the area of exchange systems is therefore one obvious field of research. The rejection of a hypothesis can sometimes be more informative than non-rejection—I hesitate to say 'acceptance', since although the pattern may fit the explanation, there may be other explanations which suit just as well. The models that I have put forward are not to be dismissed merely because they do not fit in one situation; rather, they provide a framework for analysing many early coin-using societies, such as the classical world, or colonial America where we have historical and anthropological information with which to compare our archaeological data. We have only just started to begin modelling the nuances of different situations (Collis, in preparation).

And what of the historical paradigm? In certain areas it has something to contribute, especially, for instance, where distributions are clearly being affected by political factors. But I wonder how many more papers will appear on 'The Catuvellauni—indigenous or invader?', a question I believe archaeology is incapable of answering, especially in our present state of ignorance of the relationship between archaeological data and ethnicity. These historical debates are little more than a statement of opinion by individual scholars: there is nothing that can be tested, proved, or disproved. The historical school may argue that 'archaeology is history or it is nothing'—many of us would disagree.

Appendix

In Rodwell's article of 1976 there are a number of areas of fact and opinion in which we disagree, and on which I would like to comment briefly:

Winchester   There is no acceptable evidence for a major settlement here in the Late Iron Age (*pace* Rodwell 1976, 282; Cunliffe 1976). Virtually all the Late Iron Age pottery finds have been published recently (Collis 1978), and Martin Biddle and I are in agreement that there is an occupation gap of 50 if not 150 years between the Middle Iron Age defended settlement and the early Roman town. The site may have been occupied by a number of small farm settlements, and the stray coin finds would be consistent with that (Collis 1971a). The 'debris of mint' consists of a single fragment of coin mould from a Saxon deposit.

Silchester   I can merely repeat that the dykes at Silchester are undated: they could be Iron Age, Roman, or sub-Roman (Rodwell 1976, 334).

Colchester   My summary of this site was an accurate account of the published sources available at the time I wrote (Collis 1975), except for my misplacement of the Roman fortress (Rodwell 1976, 332).

Minting   Rodwell accuses me of stating that 'Tasciovanus, Addedomaros, Dubnovellaunos and Sego . . . were *all* minting coins together in Camulodunum' (Rodwell 1976, 282–3). I only suggested that *some* of them were (Collis 1971a, 76, lines 22–3), an opinion I still hold.

Potin coinage   I do not understand Rodwell's criticisms (1976, 207–8). My attempt to use site associations to demonstrate that potin coinage enjoyed a status similar to silver and was later downgraded to that of bronze was suggestive but statistically inconclusive (Collis 1974, 1). In view of the debate at present raging in France on the date and status of potin coinage (unpublished!) it is a possibility still worth bearing in mind.

Hoard dates   Rodwell (1976, 200) suggests that there is independent dating for potin coinage. This is not so (Allen 1971, 131). The early dating proposed by Allen is now generally accepted, on the evidence of associations in Britain (Snettisham, Caburn), but his fixed point for absolute dating was the assumption that the potin hoards were associated with the Caesarean campaign. His dating cannot therefore be used to date the hoards! Likewise, we should note that the dating of our Gallo-Belgic series is based on the one fixed point in the Gallic coinage, the Caesarean conquest. This only provides a *terminus ante quem* and much longer chronologies could be proposed which would extend the date range of the British hoards (eg Snettisham). Equally, we cannot use the 'date' of Snettisham to date all other finds in similar art style to the same couple of years: the style could have been in vogue for a century. The historical premises for the dating of the Gallic coinage are no longer acceptable, and in any case the whole argument is circular. The 'Caesarean hoards' mapped by Rodwell (1976, fig 8) may cover at least half a century.

Coin statistics   In his appendix (Rodwell 1976, 313–15), Rodwell claims to have disproved my statistics on the ratio of gold to bronze from various sites. However, his grouping of sites is different from mine: he is mainly comparing my 'major market' and 'minor market' categories which I have always considered to have similar ratios, as his statistics confirm. It is my third category of minor sites/stray finds which is different, having a much higher percentage of gold. As stated above, this hypothesis has still to be tested against good site data, but there are indications that there may be something in it. I doubt if it is due merely to sampling bias (a matter discussed in Collis 1971, 77; *pace* Rodwell 1976, 313).

'Forged' coins   There seem to be three possible interpretations to be placed on plated bronze coins: 1. that they are tokens (unlikely); 2. that they were recognized as forgeries and were used as bronze (Collis 1974); 3. that they were more easily passed on market sites (Rodwell 1976, 316–17). On the whole I think there is an element in truth in both of the latter suggestions. However we should note that dishonesty in trading is not something confined to market forms of exchange, but is also found in 'gift exchange'. Sahlins (1972) notes that cheating is rife where 'distance' is greatest either in geographical or kinship terms, and it also helps to explain the phenomenon noted by Rodwell that finds of 'forgeries' are more common on the periphery of the main distribution of a coin type.

Bibliography

Allen, D F, 1971 British potin coins: a review, in Jesson, M, & Hill, D (eds), *The Iron Age and its hill-forts*, 127–56

Collis, J R, 1971a Functional and theoretical interpretations of British coinage, *World Archaeol*, **3**, 71–84

Collis, J R, 1971b Markets and money, in Jesson, M & Hill, D (eds), *The Iron Age and its hill-forts*, 97–103

Collis, J R, 1974a A functionalist approach to pre-Roman coinage, in Casey, J & Reece, R (eds), *Coins and the archaeologist*, 1–11

Collis J R, 1974b Data for dating, in *ibid*, 73–83

Collis J R, 1975 *Defended sites of the Late La Tène in Central and Western Europe*

Collis J R, 1978, *Winchester excavations, 2,: Excavations in the suburbs and the western part of the town*

Collis J R, 1980 Aulnat and urbanization in France: a second interim report, *Archaeol J*, **137**

Collis J R, in preparation A typology of coin distributions, *World Archaeol*

Cunliffe, B W, 1976 The origins of urbanisation in Britain, in Cunliffe, B W & Rowley, R T, (eds), *Oppida in barbarian Europe*, 135–622

Harding, D W, 1974 *The Iron Age in Lowland Britain*

Megaw, J V S, Collis, J R & Spratling, M G, 1973 Gussage All Saints: discussion, *Antiquity*, **47**, 306–8

Polanyi, K, *et al* (eds), 1957 *Trade and market in the early empires: economies in history and theory*

Rodwell, W J, 1976 Coinage, oppida, and the rise of Belgic power in south-eastern Britain, in Cunliffe, B W & Rowley, R T (eds), *Oppida in barbarian Europe*, 181–366

Sahlins, M, 1972 *Stone Age economics*

Tournaire, J, Büchsenschütz, O, Henderson, J, Collis, J & Périchon, R, in preparation Moules à flan monétaire en France

Wainwright, G J, Spratling, M, 1973 The Iron Age settlement of Gussage All Saints, *Antiquity*, **47**, 117–30

Iron Age coinage: a counter reply   *Warwick Rodwell*

Dr Collis's observations on my 1976 paper emphasize our differences of approach to the study of Celtic coinage and to the whole realm of data interpretation in archaeology. For the most part the differences are irreconcilable and continued discussion will be sterile, although the keen critic will doubtless observe that we both stray into the opposite camp from time to time, when lured by some attractive idea. I firmly believe that archaeology is a means to an end, and that the end-product is history.

It is an over-simplification to divide scholars into the 'traditional' and 'new' schools: Allen, Harding, and myself have all been assigned to the former, yet there are fundamental differences between our approaches. For example, I have never made any *general* assertion that 'Gallo-Belgic coins reflect invasion'. At the opposite end of the spectrum it is easy to say that coin-using spread 'by adoption', but there has to be a driving force for this to happen: 'adoption' is not a passive state, or a natural phenomenon like rain. As soon as we try to explain the manufacture, use, or distribution of an artefact we begin to write history. It matters little whether this embryonic history is dubbed social, political, or economic: it is still equally incapable of proof in anything approaching a scientific sense. Like it or not, in the long run opinion does rule.

Collis asks four 'simple questions', all socio-economic, and all valid in their own terms. But archaeological evidence simply cannot be used to answer such questions. We all agree that model building does not provide answers, but may suggest them: so does deductive argument. Admittedly, at its worst, the 'traditional' approach involves the asking of specific historical questions, followed by their attempted answering with archaeologial evidence. That blinkered approach patently will not do. Inductive reasoning, properly used, should take a body of data and compare and contrast it with similar bodies of data from other periods in the same general location, or with contemporary material from an adjacent area, to see whether common themes and patterns emerge. Several interpretations may suggest themselves, all of which should be stated, even if the researcher has a preference for one. If the preferred interpretation seems to have a bearing on recorded history, let it be so stated and explored.

Deductive reasoning subsumes a variety of approaches too, and sounds to be an attractive concept as defined by Collis. In practice, however, it tends to lead off in two unsatisfactory directions. First, there are those who indulge in verbose and contorted circumlocutions to demonstrate something which is devastatingly obvious to others who have used their iniquitous assets of perception, induction, logic and sheer common-sense. Secondly, there are those whose deductive reasoning involves the building of models from a hotch-potch of quaint but irrelevant data. To try to shed light on Iron Age Britain by taking models from Classical Greece, Colonial America, or tropical Africa is, I submit, a largely pointless exercise, a mere intellectual game. A model constructed on a set of circumstances remote in time or place may well be found to 'fit' the subject of enquiry, but how relevant is it? As a colleague once remarked, 'you can iron your shirt in an olive press, but that's not what it's made for'. If a chain of communication can be reconstructed to link Iron Age Britain with Colonial America, or wherever, then a model built around the known use of coinage in the one place *might* shed light on the other. But to forge the links of that chain a lot of deductive reasoning is going to be needed.

An example, outside coinage, will serve to illustrate the specious and irrelevant strands which can be introduced into an argument in the name of inductive thinking. If we constructed models for the use of circular stones and fired-clay lumps with central perforations, a vast number of possibilities could be assembled. A glance across the world would show that they had many mundane uses, such as weights for looms, thatch, fishing nets, and clock ropes, as well as exotic applications, such as 'beer-pouring stones' (rings through which libations were poured into graves). Somewhere they have perhaps been used as bakers' models for doughnuts and countless other curious applications. Which hypothesis would we advance as best fitting the evidence in Britain (especially for the considerable number of rings which have been found close to hearths)?

This example might be dismissed as flippant, but the principle enunciated and the dangers highlighted here are real enough. I still believe that inductive reasoning and hypothesizing are, in the long run, likely to bring us to a truer understanding of the British Iron Age than deductive approaches. Meanwhile, John Collis and I have agreed to differ: this is healthy and prevents stagnation.

A computer-based information storage and retrieval scheme for Iron Age coin finds in Britain?
Colin Haselgrove and John Collis

In a volume which brings together the results of recent research into the origins and development of coinage in north-west Europe, we hope it will not seem entirely out of place to include a short paper addressed to one aspect of the future data requirements of archaeologists and numismatists active in this particular field of study—the possibility of establishing and operating a computer-based information storage and retrieval system for Iron Age coin finds in Britain. Clearly this is far too complex an issue, both technically and ethically, for us to explore all the possible implications of such a proposal in the space available to us and we would not wish to make any such claim; our purpose in writing this note is to do no more than to outline the case for designing such a system as we see it in the hope that this will encourage comment and criticism and open up as wide a discussion as possible before any attempt is made to finalize the form of a computer-based record. We shall therefore be reviewing in turn the factors which lead us to advocate such a step, the potential lines of analysis that such a record would facilitate, and finally the kinds of information one would want to include and the overall relationship we envisage between this scheme and conventional data records.

We should, however, preface this discussion with a disclaimer. As archaeologists, our work to date has been concerned not so much with the study of Iron Age coins *per se*, but rather with the question of what could be learnt about their significance and use in the context of the prehistoric societies that manufactured them. In particular, we have been concerned with the kinds of information which can be extracted from an analysis of the contexts within which we find the coins on archaeological sites, their associations with other artefact categories, and from their stratification, and from the study of their geographical distribution, both in relation to one another and to other factors such as site hierarchy, river systems, soil potential, etc. It is in this respect that we have encountered serious difficulties in collating the necessary data. We mention this simply because any form of information storage system involves the selection of as many as possible of the data relevant to the analyses one envisages being performed on them and the exclusion, implicitly or explicitly, of the remainder. We shall return to this question below; for the moment it suffices to make the point that maximum progress in this field will come about only through the combination of the information adduced by numismatists from the study of the coins and their inter-relationships with that obtained by archaeologists in relating this body of data to various other aspects of the archaeological record. What is needed in effect is an information storage system which seeks to avoid bias in the direction of either archaeology or numismatics and instead by its very existence offers a bridge between the two areas of study and encourages scholars of either persuasion to explore hitherto neglected aspects of what is after all the material output of the *same* prehistoric societies.

Present problems

Having said this, let us consider the scale of the problem which led both of us independently to the conclusion that the establishment of a computer-based information storage

and retrieval system needed urgent consideration. When the late Derek Allen published his gazetteer of find-spots of Celtic coins in Britain in 1960, it brought together information relating to approximately 10 000 provenances (Allen 1960). Nearly twenty years later, as a result of the upsurge in the number of excavations conducted and of the increased scale of human interference with the landscape in general, it has proved possible to add information relating to nearly 2 500 further provenances (Haselgrove 1978; in preparation), while over the same period of time, Scheers (1977) has revolutionized our knowledge of the find patterns of the continental members of some of the earliest series found in Britain. Thus, even if one excludes the 3 000 odd coins from a single exceptional site, Hengistbury Head (Cunliffe 1978), we possess information relating to something in excess of 9 500 provenances, of which approximately 58% are hoard finds, 13% are site finds (whether from excavations or as surface finds from known sites), and the remaining 29% are scattered, often single, chance finds. In view of the number of finds, the information presented in the gazetteers is, understandably, kept to a minimum: county, parish, NGR, date, type, reference, owner, and additional cases. In many cases the association of the coin with other archaeological material is not even indicated.

The importance of Allen's work, and before him that of G C Brooke and Sir John Evans, in collating and publishing all this information cannot be overstressed: without it, the task of modern scholars would be daunting indeed. However, this cannot be used to obscure the fact that the use of the published gazetteers can present very considerable difficulties, particularly for the archaeologist whose interest lies in contextual information. The coins are listed in the gazetteers according to their type, and the outcome of this is that if someone wants to compile a list of coins found at a particular site, to reconstruct the contents of an otherwise unpublished hoard in detail, or to study the coins found in a particular area, he has to search through some hundreds of pages in meticulous detail. Moreover, if one's interest lies in a more detailed analysis than this, eg in the associations of different types of coin with other cultural material, the functional context in which coins were lost or discarded, or the patterns of coin loss on a site during different phases of its occupation, the problem is magnified several-fold by the need to consult a wide range of published material, often several reports for a single site, and in some cases, at least, obscure and difficult to consult locally.

The use of the computer to store very large amounts of information and to produce it on request or to relate various data items to one another, has been well covered elsewhere (eg Doran & Hodson 1975) and need not be discussed further here. However, despite the obvious potential of the computer as a tool for the quick and effective exploration of this body of data, there are clearly a number of other questions which need to be looked at before the initial outlay of time and money can be justified, not least the possibility that existing arrangements could be modified to serve roughly the same function. The record that comes nearest to fulfilling this condition is the Index of Celtic Coins maintained at the Institute of Archaeology, Oxford. At present this contains cards with details and photographs for something over 3 000 British coins, of which less than half have known find-spots, although it is probable that many of the now unprovenanced coins are in fact recorded as find-spots lacking a traceable coin in the gazetteers. However, although it provides indispensable background information on individual coin finds, and indeed could be greatly expanded in this role, the very bulk of the Index mitigates against its use for the quick retrieval of most categories of information, while the service it provides is necessarily restricted to those able to visit Oxford in person. Broadly speaking, we feel that the Index must be considered as an adjunct of detailed research rather than as a centralized store of information which can efficiently handle the answering of queries on an *ad hoc* basis. Certainly, the Index cannot rival a computer-based information storage system in terms of flexibility of access, the ability to supply information on demand in a wide range of formats—print-out, on-line or in a machine-readable medium—or even in the case of updating the record of particular finds or adding new material.

The question of updating the record and attempting to keep abreast of the impact of new finds on existing interpretations leads us to two further arguments in favour of a computerized format. New finds continue to accumulate at an almost frightening rate—over 400 have been noted since March 1977 (Haselgrove, in preparation) —and this is only the tip of the iceberg. No one will wish to wait a further twenty years for the publication of a new supplementary gazetteer, which will in any case contain only a proportion of the information relating to each find, while in the present and probable future climate of financial restrictions, the alternative of including an annual note in a conventional publication seems far less attractive than the possibilities opened up by the computer for the dissemination of more detailed records to interested parties and institutions. Secondly, given this explosive increase of material which will result in the doubling of the number of finds in the not too distant future, we feel there is a lot to be said for making the necessary initial investment of labour and resources in creating a computerized file *now*, rather than waiting until the data mass has become totally unmanageable. However, in the final analysis the strongest argument for developing a computerized system rests in the kinds of approach to data analysis beginning to be adopted by archaeologists and numismatists and which seem likely to develop as a major focus of research effort in the foreseeable future.

Future questions

There are two headings under which future work will fall, both of which will demand much greater accessibility to and manipulation of the data. First there are the questions to be asked of the data, the models which require testing against the available information, or which need confirming through further data collection. Secondly, there is the testing of the significance of the data, in other words the question of whether there is observable bias in the data collection or whether the samples of coins from which we are arguing are statistically significant.

Up to the late 1960s, the matter of models was not particularly important, as there was virtually only one framework to deal with as far as context and distribution were concerned, and that was based on the historical paradigm. The distributions of pre-Roman coins were used exclusively in one of two ways: either to demonstrate the presence and extent of invasions if the coins were types emanating from the continent (eg Allen 1960), or to define tribal boundaries, especially using the later inscribed types (eg Allen 1944; Rodwell 1976).

In the last decade however, a number of competing, alternative 'explanations' have been proposed, suggesting that fundamentally different factors may underlie coin distributions (eg Collis 1971a). In the main, these models have stressed socio-economic factors or purely economic considerations, suggesting for instance that we may be able to identify trading patterns around individual market centres (Collis 1971b; 1976); or that coins may relate to topographical or environmental features such as soils, river systems, or Roman roads (eg Hodder & Orton 1976, 227), thus furnishing us with information about settlement patterns and networks of communication; or that the distribution of wealth within society may be a key factor We must also surely admit to knowing very little about the structure of coin distributions, which can vary from widely diffused scatters to dense concentrations, and from even distribution to disjointed ones, perhaps concentrated around and in major settlement nucleations. To attack these problems we require considerably more information than is provided by a single dot on a simple outline map, and when we realize that the 'truth' is likely to be a combination of many of the factors mentioned above, we are entering an area where even complex models and maps may be quite inadequate to convey the full subtlety of the processes going on in our ancient societies.

Turning now to the second point for discussion, there has long been a realization that there is considerable bias on our data, but so far it has been difficult to test for this owing to our lack of a really detailed study of the circumstances of discovery of the vast majority of our coins. The impact of an individual collector, the proximity of a museum, present-day land usage, or the methods of retrieval in use on an excavated site can all affect the form of a distribution map as we know it (Haselgrove, in preparation; Rodwell, above pp 43–52). Laux's survey of the pattern of discovery of Bronze Age finds on the Lüneburg Heath (quoted in Hodder & Orton 1976, 21–3) neatly demonstrates how the historical process of data accumulation fundamentally affects distributions and so our interpretation of them from one generation to another.

It has been argued in an earlier paper (Collis 1974) that we might usefully consider the processes by which the coinage of an ancient society finally reaches our museums in terms of a hierarchy of samples, each biased by various factors as we descend from one level to the next and representing an overall loss of information in its lower stages. In simplified terms, these levels are: 'coins minted', 'coins circulating', 'coins lost or discarded', and 'coins found'. The biases we noted above related to the discrepancy between 'coins lost' and 'coins found', but to take examples from the higher levels, the status, function, and location of a site will obviously affect the coins reaching and 'circulating' on it, whereas the size and value of the coins and their frequency of handling will be the principal factors determining which of them are lost or concealed. The most elusive of these levels and potentially the most interesting, is perhaps 'coins circulating', which might be approached jointly by numismatists calculating 'coins minted' (eg Allen 1975) and by the archaeologist working from 'coins found', although this re-emphasizes the need for us to eliminate, or at least allow for bias in our data, as the numismatist in his attempt to reconstruct the patterns of 'coins minted', is dependent on the small fraction which constitute the sample of 'coins found'.

Another area of debate is the significance of presence and absence. A blank on a coin distribution map may mean many things: a lack of fieldwork, an area uninhabited in the Iron Age, or one that could not get or did not want coins, or that was using other coin types. To test these different possibilities we need to compare the coin data with other archaeological material, and especially the distribution of one coin type against another, as well as testing to see whether our sample sizes are sufficiently large for absence to be judged significant. Other typical problems include deciding whether the ratios of gold to bronze coins on a certain site or in a defined area are significantly different from another site or region, or whether the mode of discovery is different from one area to another. These are questions which can mostly be answered by standard procedures such as those provided by SPSS (Nie et al 1975), once the data are in suitable form. Given that the data are increasing from year to year, and given that the questions we wish to ask of them are becoming ever more complex, the case for computerization seems overwhelming.

Proposed programme

With the above points in mind, let us turn in conclusion to the question of what configuration a general purpose information storage and retrieval system for Iron Age coin finds might assume. As we have already stressed, it is one thing to devise a scheme for the storage and retrieval of information selected by oneself with a particular programme of analysis in mind, and quite another to anticipate every demand which may be made on such a system in the future. Thus, although we have tried to suggest some of the likely preoccupations of the 1980s, we are only too conscious in putting forward our ideas that we have had to rely largely on our own experience of what is likely to be required. It is inevitable that some points of importance will have been overlooked and will be brought up in the wider discussion that we hope this paper will open up.

Our suggestion, then, is that each recorded coin find should be given a unique number, with new finds being added to the list consecutively. This would allow the computerized record to take the form of a series of separately stored, but interlocking, files with access between them being maintained solely by the coin number and file number. As regards the actual configuration of these files we would envisage at least six basic units (Fig 37), which may be briefly characterized as follows:

1 **Basic record** This would include the fundamental details of the coin, its type according to existing classifications, weight, diameter, dominant metal, certainty of identification, and obverse and reverse die numbers, which like the coin number would be unique. Other information would include the county, parish and national grid reference for the find, the latter accurate to twelve figures where known to allow the investigation of within-site patterns of loss and discard.

2 **Context** Where relevant and available, this file would include the name of the site or hoard from which a coin derived, the date and nature of its excavation context, the type of find and how it was made, and the nature of any associated artefacts. Also listed would be information relating to the nature and function of the site, such as its topographical situation, the proximity of communication arteries, and the soil zone within which it is located.

3 **Coin history** The purpose of this file is to record the history of the coin since its discovery, including the date of discovery, changes of ownership, its present location or fate, availability for study, and published references. It is hoped that this sort of information will allow coins that turn up on the market to be matched with 'lost' finds, thus confirming their authenticity. Obviously access to this file would have to be limited in certain cases for reasons of security.

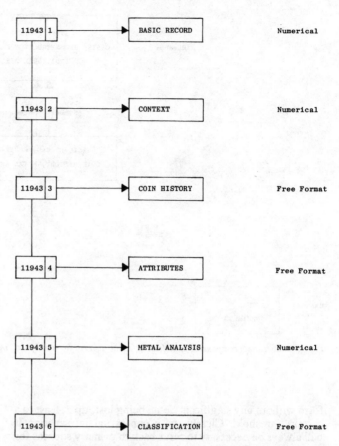

Fig 37 Basic units of computer-based storage and retrieval scheme for prehistoric coin finds in Britain

4 **Attributes** While the work of Allen (1960 etc) and other scholars has gone a long way towards establishing the basic relationships between Iron Age coin types, there are still many areas of uncertainty. By recording the presence of attributes other than those included in the *Basic record*, it is hoped that this file will enable one to challenge the validity of existing taxonomies and also to explore the extent to which particular motifs have an identity which transcends the types on which they occur. In conjunction with *Basic record* and *Metal analysis*, this file should permit the application of various kinds of numerical data analysis as outlined by, for example, Doran and Hodson (1975).

5 **Metal analysis** Under this heading would be included specific gravity determinations, the results of physical methods of analysis in terms of proportions of major, minor, and trace elements present, and details of the analytical method chosen.

6 **Classification** This file would be available to receive the results of fresh attempts at classification and also information on prototypes, sources of inspiration, and so on; also published reference to such work.

This characterization of the projected contents has been in no way exhaustive. There are, however, two further points which might be mentioned, the first of which concerns the format of the records. Clearly, with directly measurable quantities such as weight, elemental composition, etc, the data will all be stored in numerical form. We also feel that the qualitative information stored in the *Basic record* and *Context* files can be entered entirely in numerical

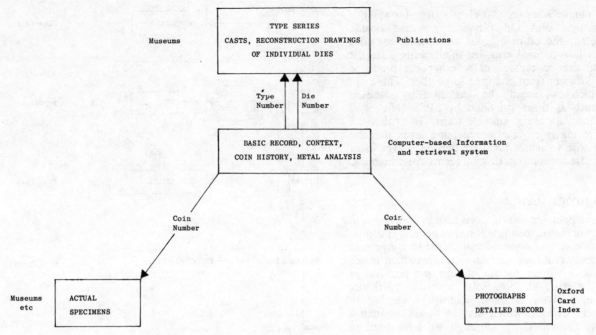

Fig 38 Interrelated components of a fully effective scheme for storage of information relating to prehistoric coin finds in Britain

form without any significant detail being lost, up at least to a certain threshold. Clearly, with contextual information it will always be necessary to refer back to primary sources for some purposes; we would hope, however, that the numerical coding together with reference contained in *Coin history* will enable the more efficient sifting of this mass of variety. The information entered in the other three files, *Coin history, Attributes,* and *Classification,* would be in alphanumeric form on some sort of free format. The second point concerns the extent to which the information it is intended to include is available and merely requires collating and coding, as opposed to having to be worked out from scratch. The situation is, in fact, relatively promising. Much of the information to be included in the *Context* file is in the process of being assembled and coded for a pilot version of this scheme (Haselgrove, in preparation), while the publication of the extensive programme of metal analysis being undertaken by Kent and his colleagues at the British Museum will fill what has hitherto been a major void. However, in other respects, such as die studies or metrological examination, the situation is frankly patchy, although a start has been made in some instances (eg Allen 1975; Mossop, in preparation; Scheers 1977), and data will have to be added on coins already listed as they become available.

We would like to stress our own belief that such a computer-based system should not be considered in isolation. There will always be instances where it is advisable, even necessary, to refer back to primary sources, whether the coins themselves, a detailed record of their find-spot or context or a representative die series. For this reason we prefer to regard the computerized segment of information as much as the linchpin of a wider system as an entity in its own right (Fig 38). Provided that a unique system of cross-referencing is maintained by *coin number* or *die number,* the computerized segment can act as an effective index to the contents of the wider system, however dispersed they are geographically. One has the technology for such a scheme; the other critical ingredient will, of course, be cooperation between individuals and institutions, for however much future technological

developments make it possible to computerize information which can at present only be maintained in another medium —one wonders about the possibility of storing images of a representative die series—the coins themselves are difficult to assemble in one place and scholars will always be dependent on the goodwill of their owners.

As regards a possible location for this data bank, we would like to put forward the case for Oxford. The Institute of Archaeology there already houses the Index of Celtic Coins referred to above, while the Ashmolean Museum is one of the major clearing houses for information relating to new discoveries, and between them, these institutions could provide the necessary backup to the computerized segment, including the restriction of access to any items the owners of coins would regard as confidential. Oxford is also close to London where the national collection is housed.

We have deliberately left out any reference to a question which seems to arise whenever the idea of a computer-based information storage system is raised, ie the extent to which the rights of the group should take preference over those of the individual researcher, an issue which will certainly have to be fully discussed in connection with this scheme. However, it is our hope that with so many problems which cannot be efficiently analysed and answered by traditional approaches in view of the vast quantities of data with which one has to deal, the advent of computer technology will see some at least of the obstacles beginning to fade away.

Bibliography

Allen, D F, 1944 Belgic dynasties of Britain and their coins, *Archaeologia,* **90,** 1–46
Allen, D F, 1960 The origins of coinage in Britain: a reappraisal, in Frere, S S (ed), *Problems of the Iron Age in southern Britain,* 97–308
Allen, D F, 1975 Cunobelin's gold, *Britannia,* **6,** 1–19
Collis, J R, 1971a Functional and theoretical interpretations of British coinage, *World Archaeol,* **3,** 71–84
Collis, J R, 1971b Markets and money, in Jesson, M & Hill, D (eds), *The Iron Age and its hill-forts,* 97–104
Collis, J R, 1974 Data for dating, in Casey, P J, & Reece, R (eds), *Coins and the archaeologist,* 73–83

Collis, J R, 1976 Town and market in Iron Age Europe, in Cunliffe, B W
   & Rowley, R T (eds), *Oppida: the beginnings of urbanisation in
   barbarian Europe*, 3–24
Cunliffe, B W, 1978 *Hengistbury Head*
Doran, J E, & Hodson, F R, 1975 *Mathematics and computers in archaeo-
   logy*
Haselgrove, C C, 1978 *Supplementary gazetteer of find-spots of Celtic coins
   in Britain, Institute of Archaeology, London, Occasional Paper*, **11a**
Haselgrove, C C, in preparation *The archaeological context of Celtic
   coinage in Britain: a quantitative approach*, PhD thesis, University of
   Cambridge
Hodder, I R, & Orton C, 1976 *Spatial analysis in archaeology*
Mossop, H R, in preparation *The coinage of the Coritani*
Nie, N H, Hull, C H, Jenkins, J G, Steinbrenner, K, & Bent, D H, 1975
   Statistical Package for the Social Sciences
Rodwell, W J, 1976 Coinage, oppida and the rise of Belgic power in
   south-eastern Britain, Cunliffe, B W, & Rowley, R T (eds), *Oppida:
   the beginnings of urbanisation in barbarian Europe*, 181–366
Scheers, S, 1977 *Traité de numismatique celtique* **II:** *La Gaule Belgique*

The coin maps

A number of participants at the conference commented on the lack of up-to-date distribution maps of British coins. Derek Allen's maps, which accompanied the Ordnance Survey's *Map of Southern Britain in the Iron Age*, were compiled from data available up to 1959 and were plotted at a comparatively small scale. Since then a number of writers, most notably Rodwell*, have published maps of their own presenting that part of the data relevant to their particular theme, but no attempt has been made to produce a compre-

hensive series of maps published at a uniform scale. The need for such a series, so clearly expressed at the conference, is to some extent met by the maps offered in the following pages.

No attempt has been made to plot every coin variety but all major classes and issues are represented, the basis for the plotting being the Gazetteer of Celtic coins published by Allen in 1961 and the supplementary Gazetteer compiled by Haselgrove in 1978. The maps therefore represent the situation recorded at the time of the conference. Finds made or noted after the compilation of Haselgrove's list have not been included. The maps were compiled in the Institute of Archaeology, Oxford, with the active assistance of Warwick Rodwell and Cynthia Poole.

*Rodwell W J, 1976 Coinage, oppida and the rise of Celtic power in south-eastern Britain, in Cunliffe, B W, & Rowley, R T (eds), *Oppida: the beginnings of urbanisation in Britain*, 181–366

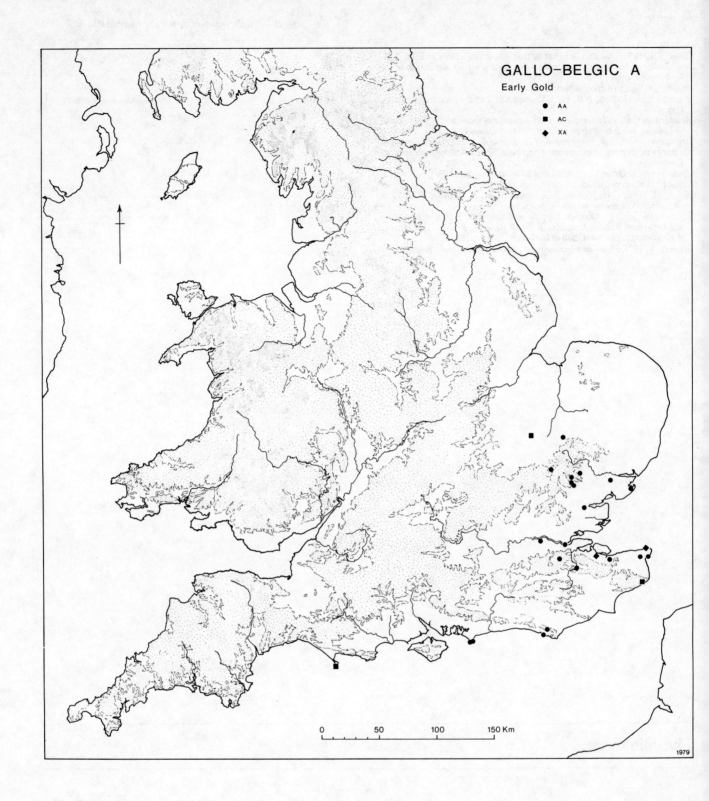

GALLO-BELGIC A
Early Gold

● AA
■ AC
◆ XA

0   50   100   150 Km

1979

Fig 39

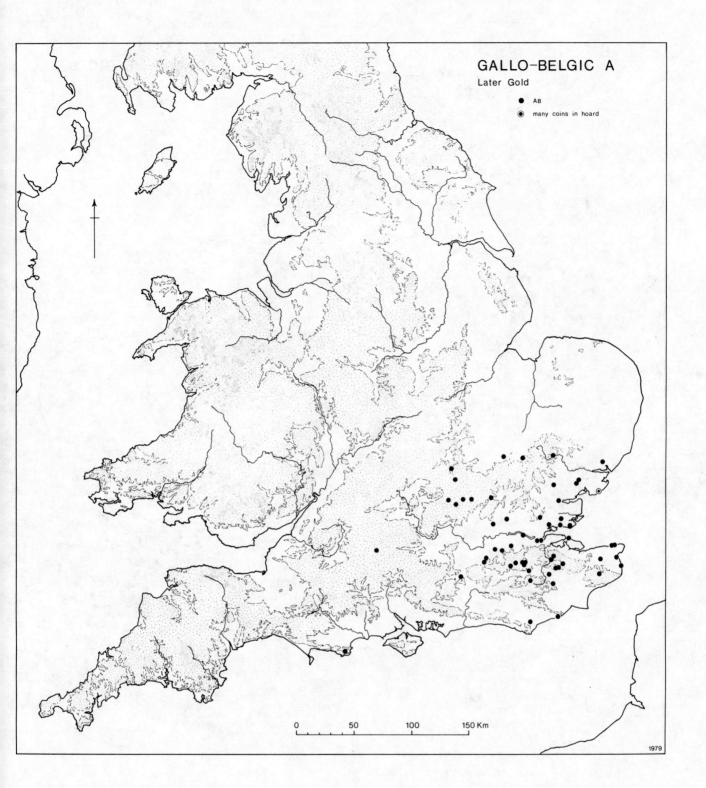

GALLO-BELGIC A

Later Gold

● AB

◉ many coins in hoard

0   50   100   150 Km

1979

Fig 40

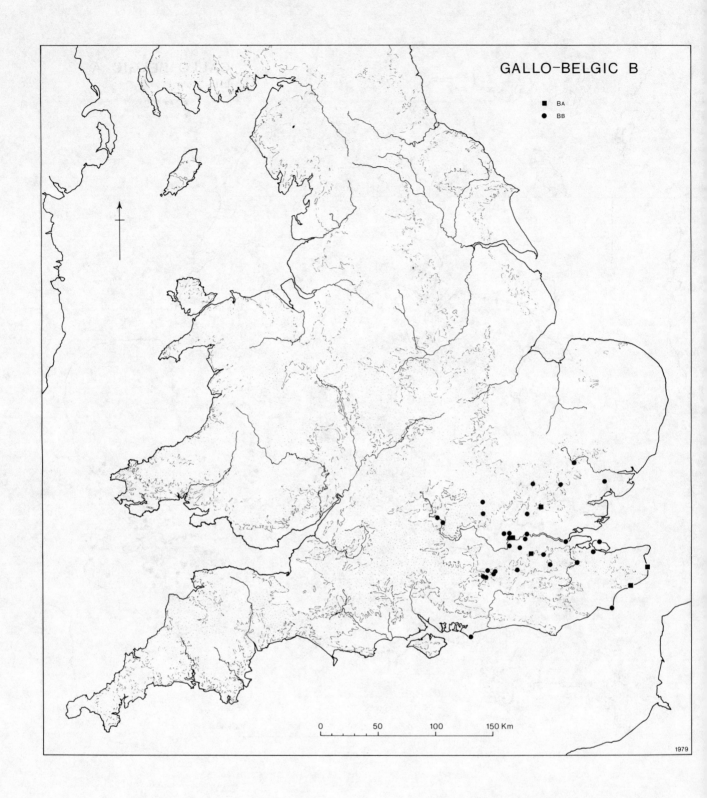

GALLO-BELGIC B

■ BA
● BB

0   50   100   150 Km

1979

Fig 41

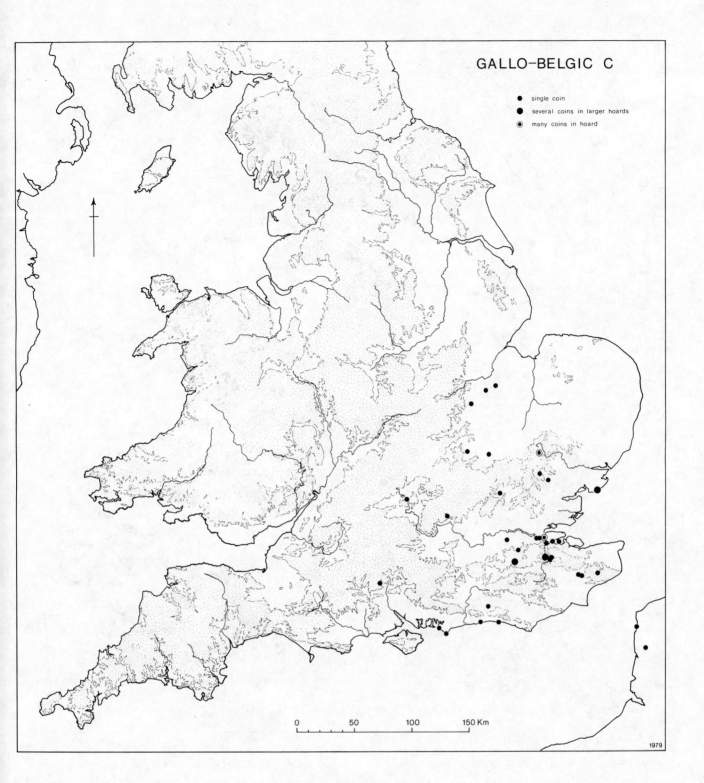

GALLO-BELGIC C

- single coin
- several coins in larger hoards
- many coins in hoard

0   50   100   150 Km

1979

Fig 42

65

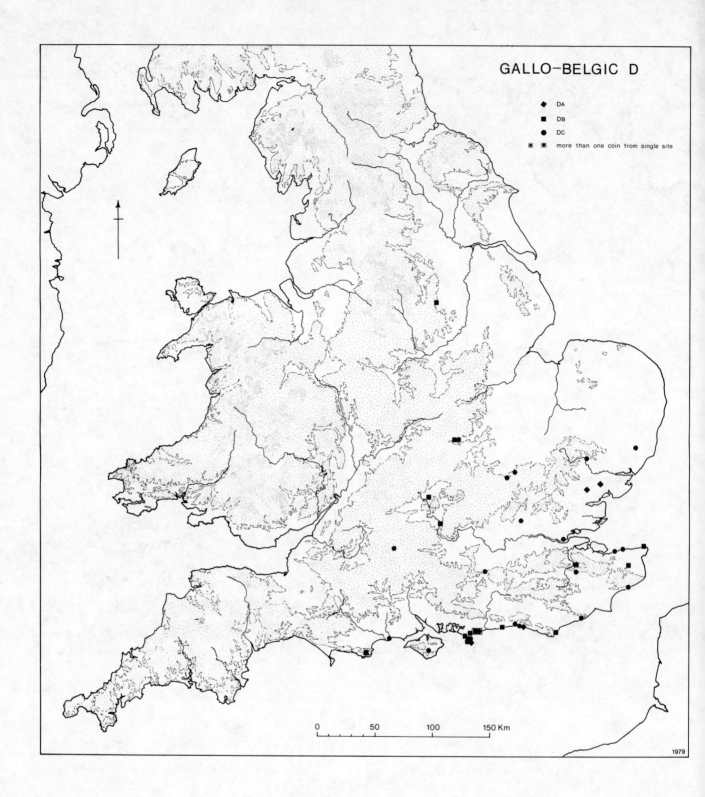

GALLO-BELGIC D

◆ DA
■ DB
● DC
▣ ◉ more than one coin from single site

0   50   100   150 Km

1979

Fig 43

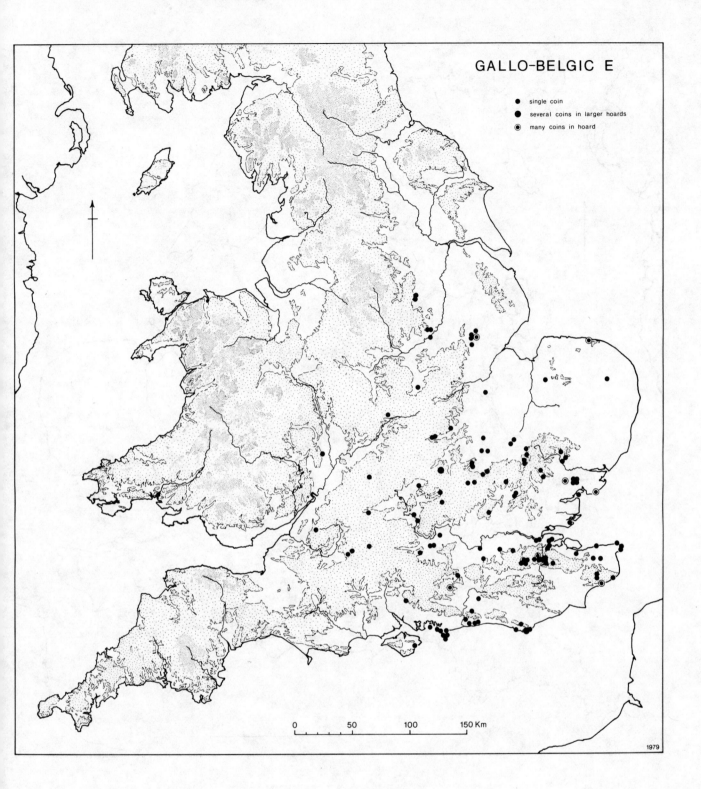

GALLO-BELGIC E

- ● single coin
- ● several coins in larger hoards
- ◉ many coins in hoard

0   50   100   150 Km

1979

Fig 44

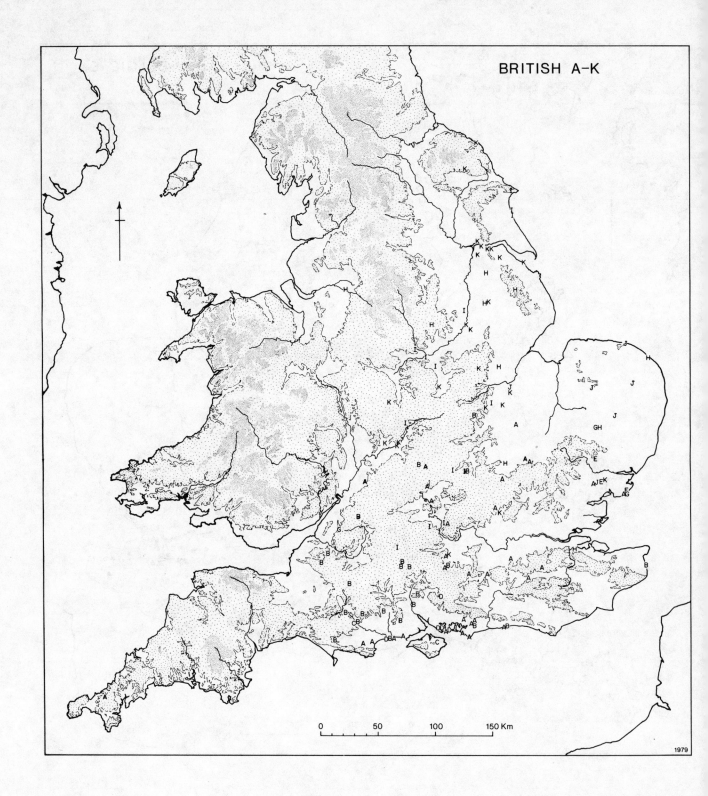

BRITISH A-K

1979

Fig 45

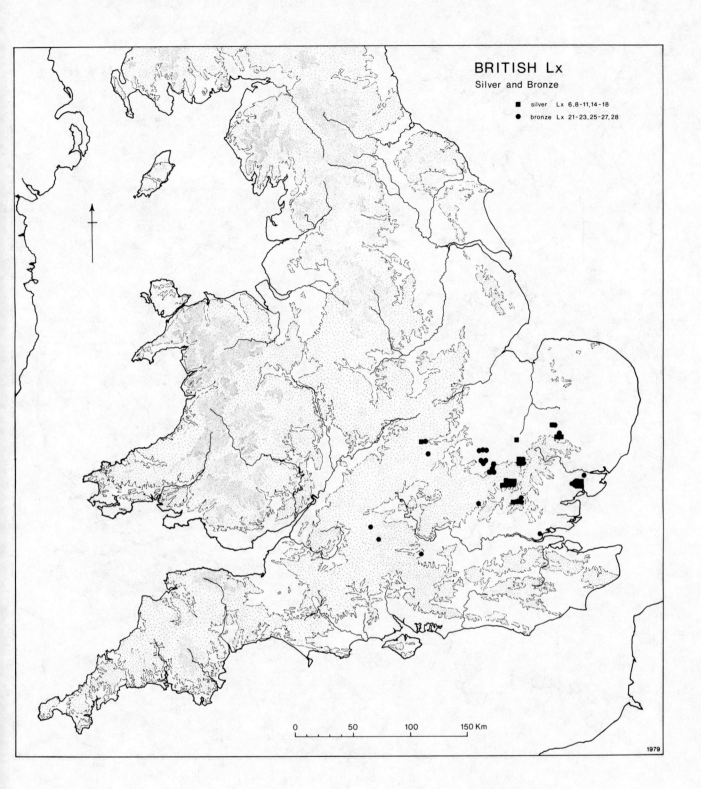

BRITISH Lx
Silver and Bronze

■ silver Lx 6,8-11,14-18
● bronze Lx 21-23,25-27,28

0   50   100   150 Km

1979

Fig 46

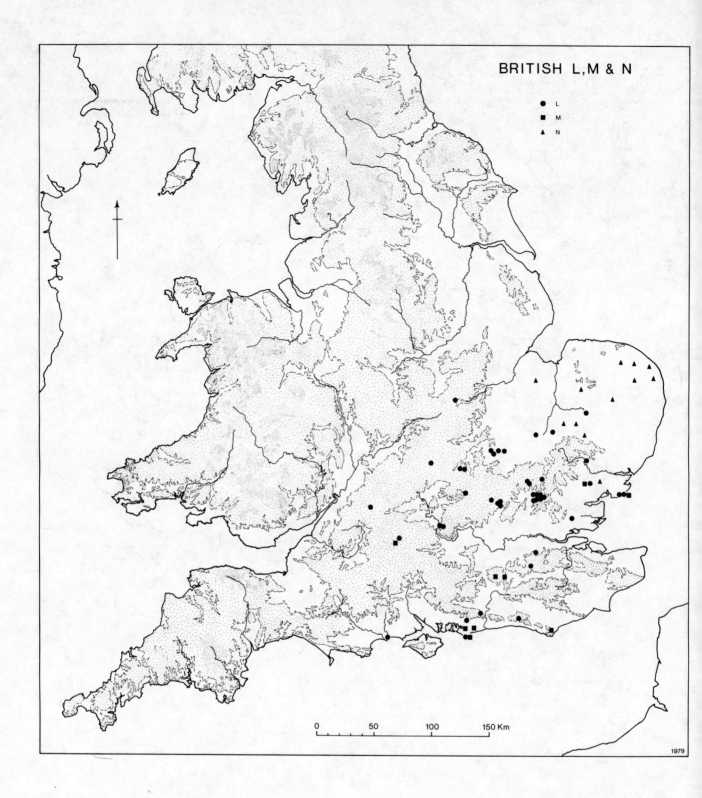

BRITISH L,M & N

● L
■ M
▲ N

0   50   100   150 Km

1979

Fig 47

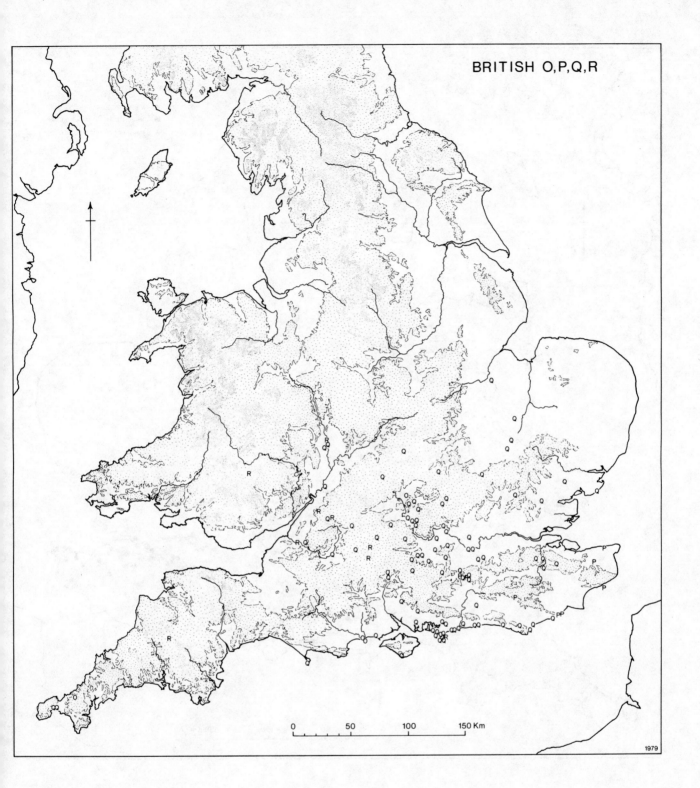

BRITISH O,P,Q,R

0   50   100   150 Km

Fig 48

71

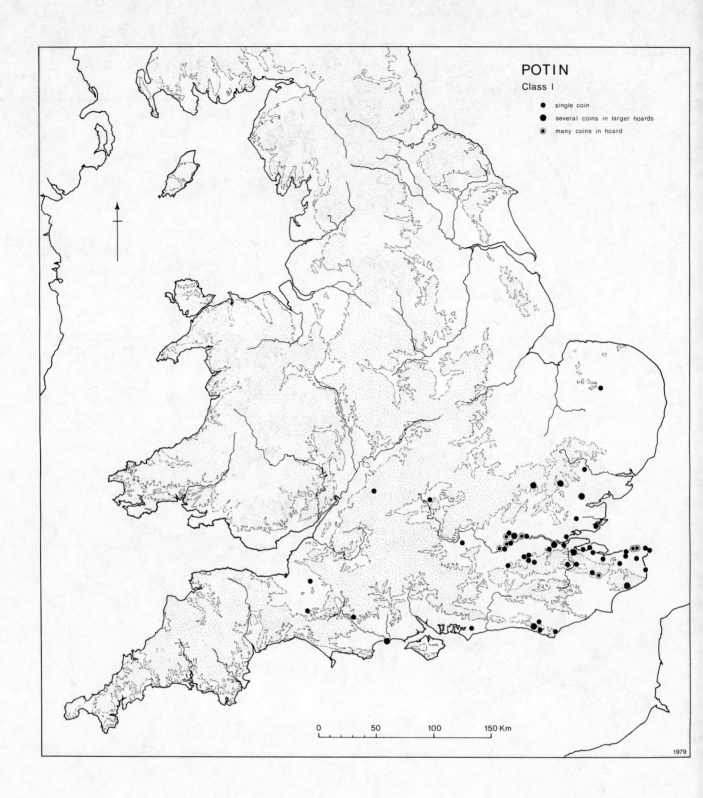

POTIN
Class I

● single coin
● several coins in larger hoards
◉ many coins in hoard

0   50   100   150 Km

1979

Fig 49

72

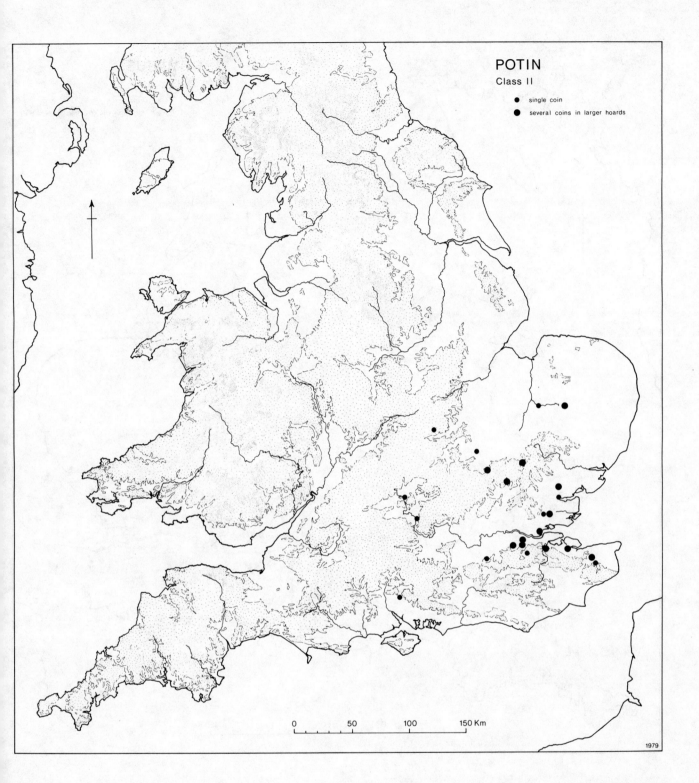

POTIN
Class II

● single coin
● several coins in larger hoards

0   50   100   150 Km

1979

Fig 50

73

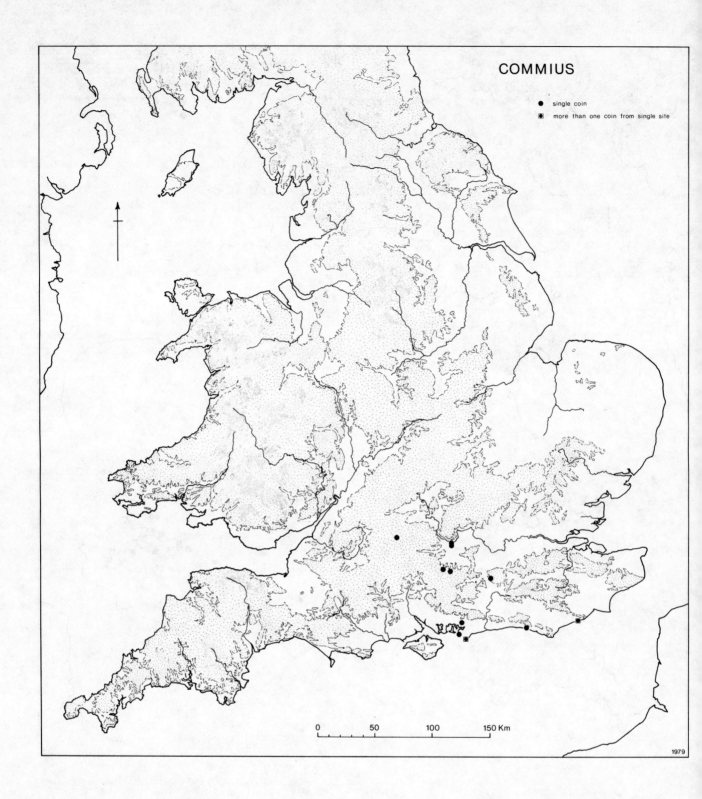

COMMIUS

● single coin
⊡ more than one coin from single site

1979

Fig 51

74

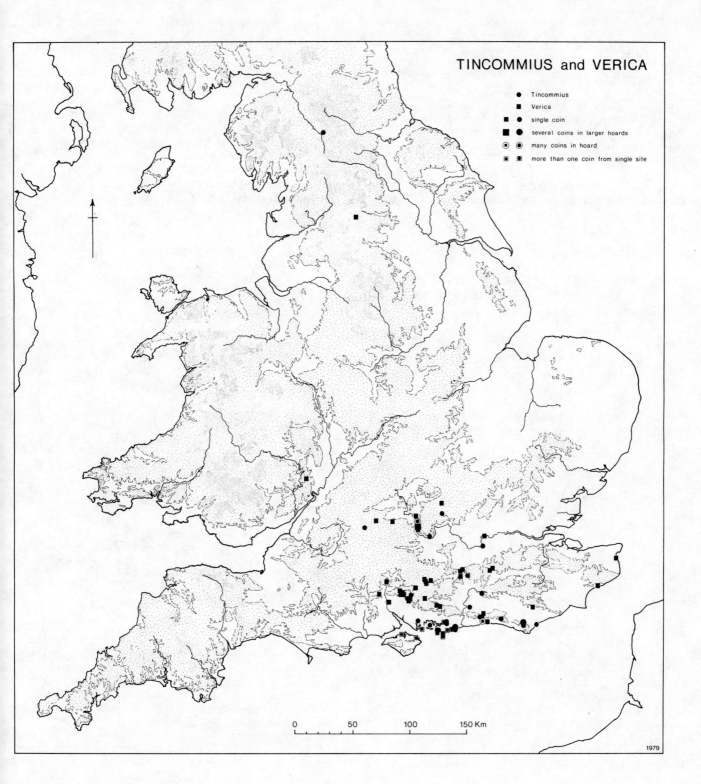

TINCOMMIUS and VERICA

- ● Tincommius
- ■ Verica
- ■ ● single coin
- ■ ● several coins in larger hoards
- ⊙ ◉ many coins in hoard
- ▣ ▣ more than one coin from single site

0   50   100   150 Km

1979

Fig 52

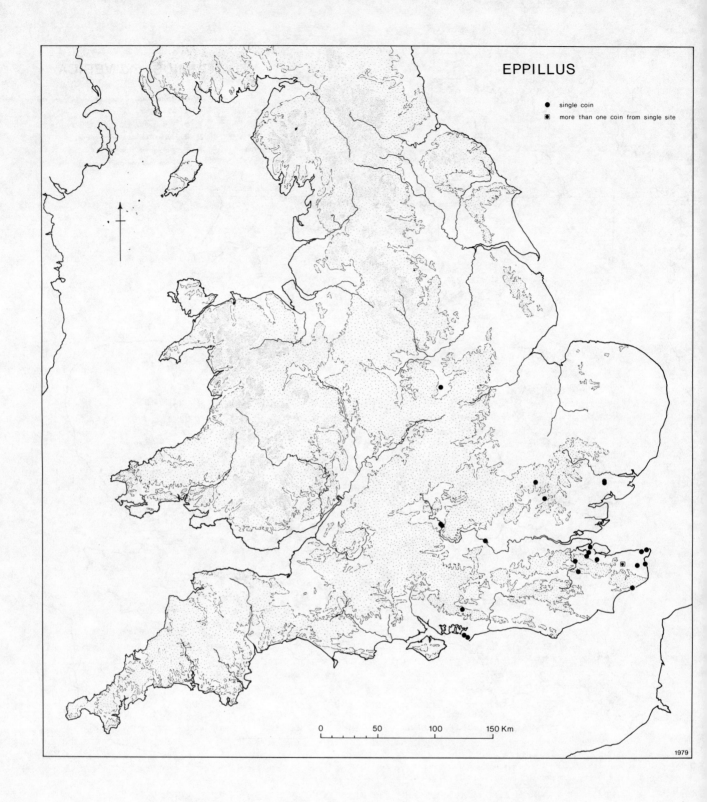

EPPILLUS

• single coin
▣ more than one coin from single site

0   50   100   150 Km

1979

Fig 53

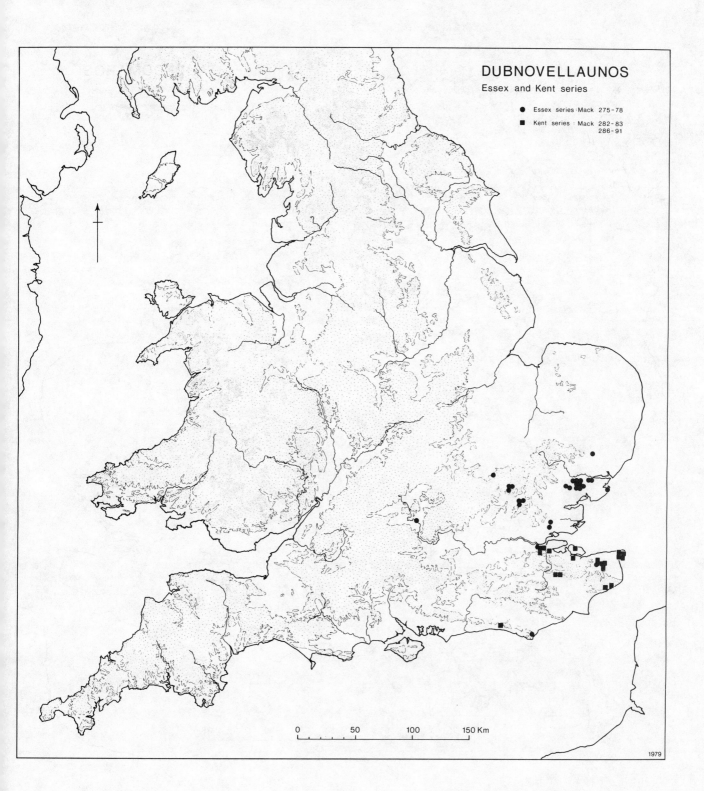

DUBNOVELLAUNOS
Essex and Kent series

● Essex series : Mack 275 – 78
■ Kent series : Mack 282 – 83
                              286 – 91

0   50   100   150 Km

1979

Fig 54

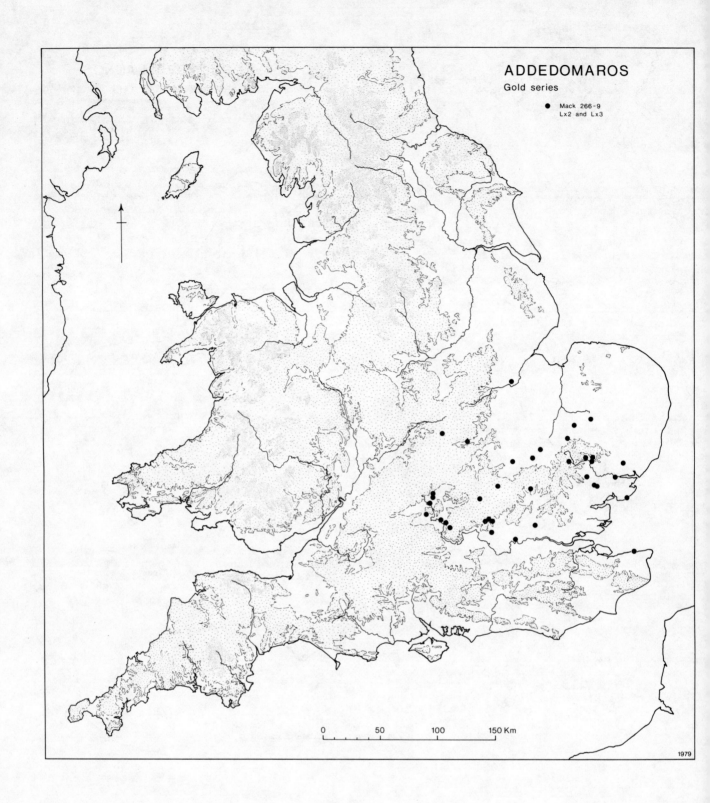

ADDEDOMAROS
Gold series

● Mack 266-9
  Lx2 and Lx3

0   50   100   150 Km

1979

Fig 55

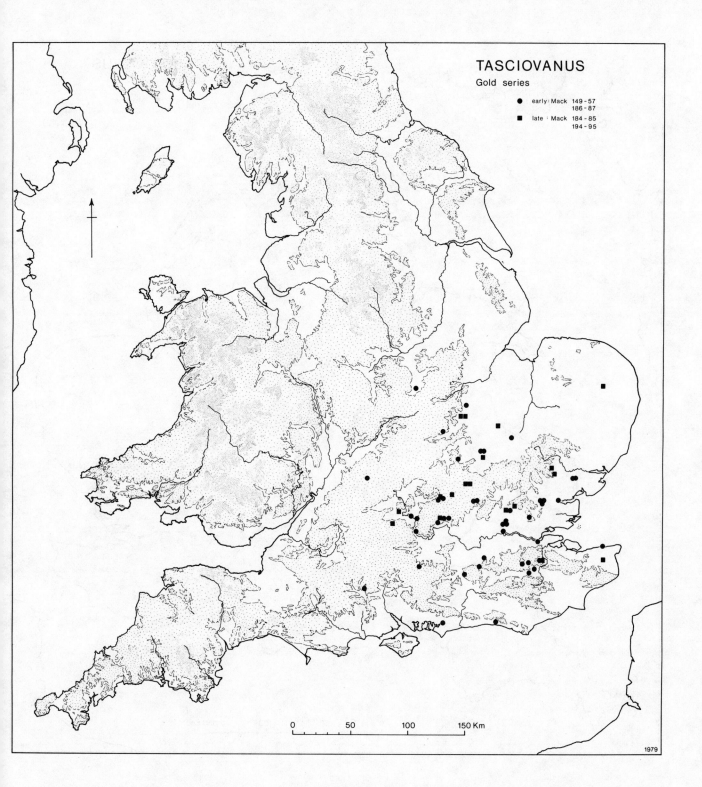

TASCIOVANUS
Gold series

● early: Mack 149 - 57
           186 - 87
■ late : Mack 184 - 85
          194 - 95

0   50   100   150 Km

1979

Fig 56

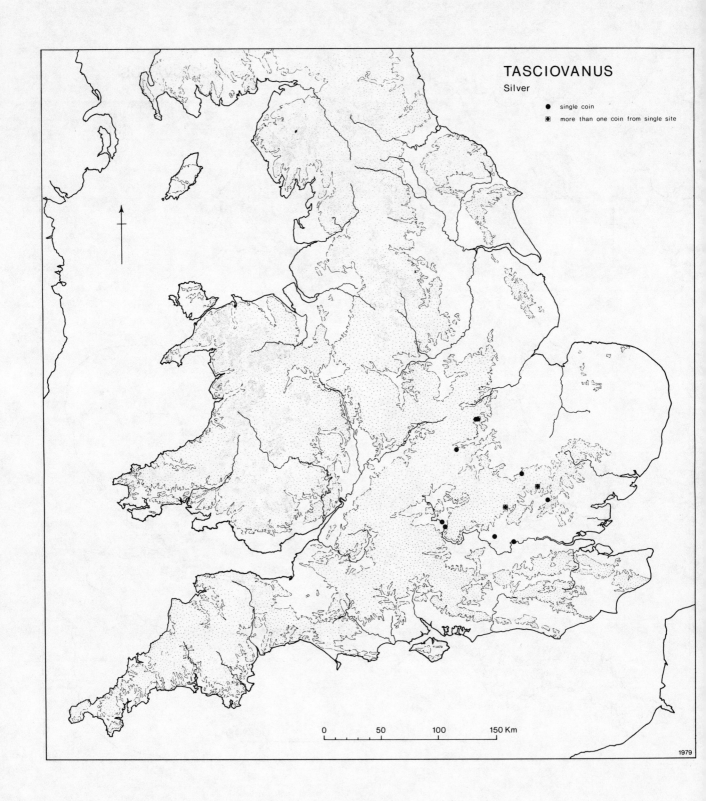

TASCIOVANUS
Silver

● single coin
▣ more than one coin from single site

0   50   100   150 Km

1979

Fig 57

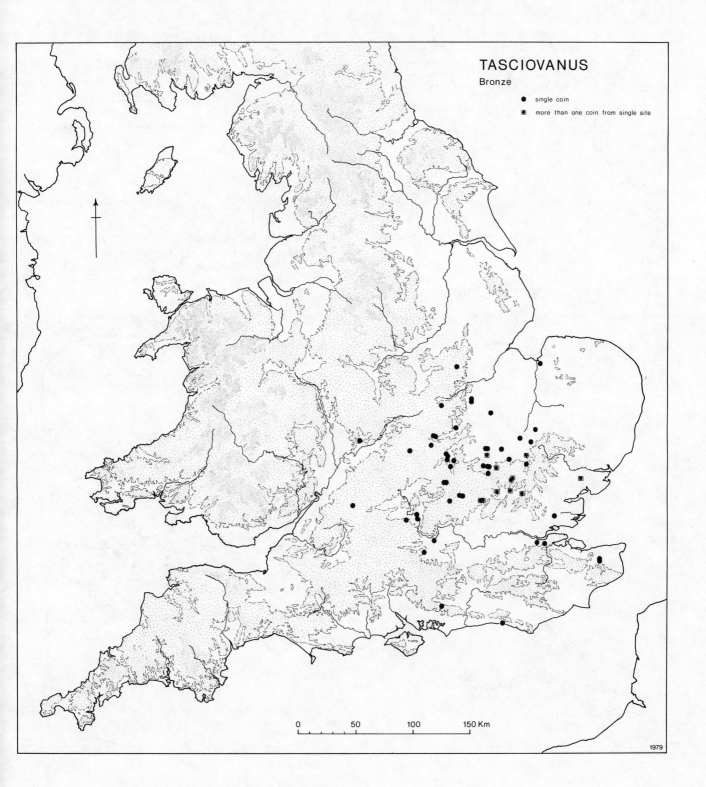

TASCIOVANUS
Bronze

● single coin

▣ more than one coin from single site

0   50   100   150 Km

1979

Fig 58

81

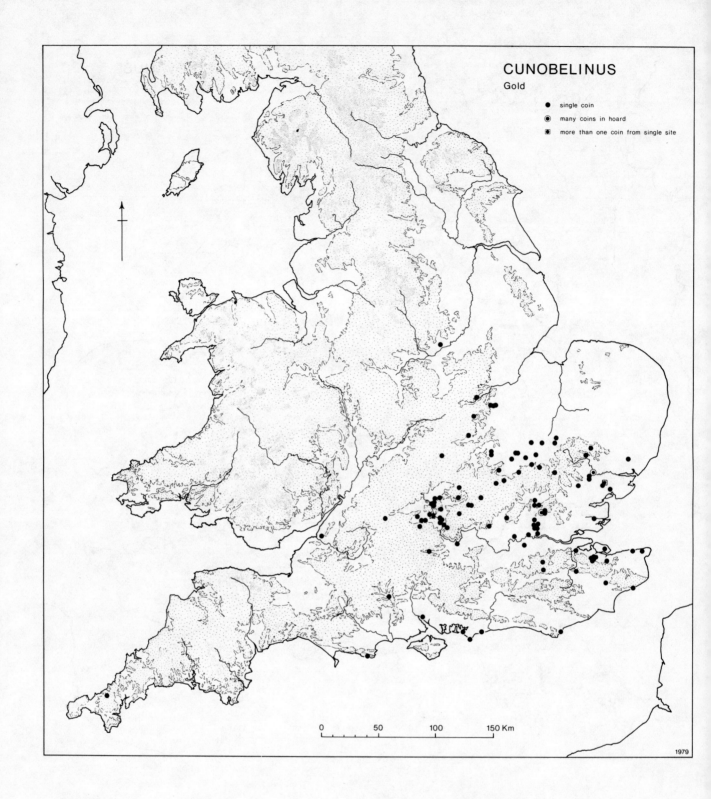

CUNOBELINUS
Gold

● single coin
◉ many coins in hoard
▣ more than one coin from single site

0   50   100   150 Km

1979

Fig 59

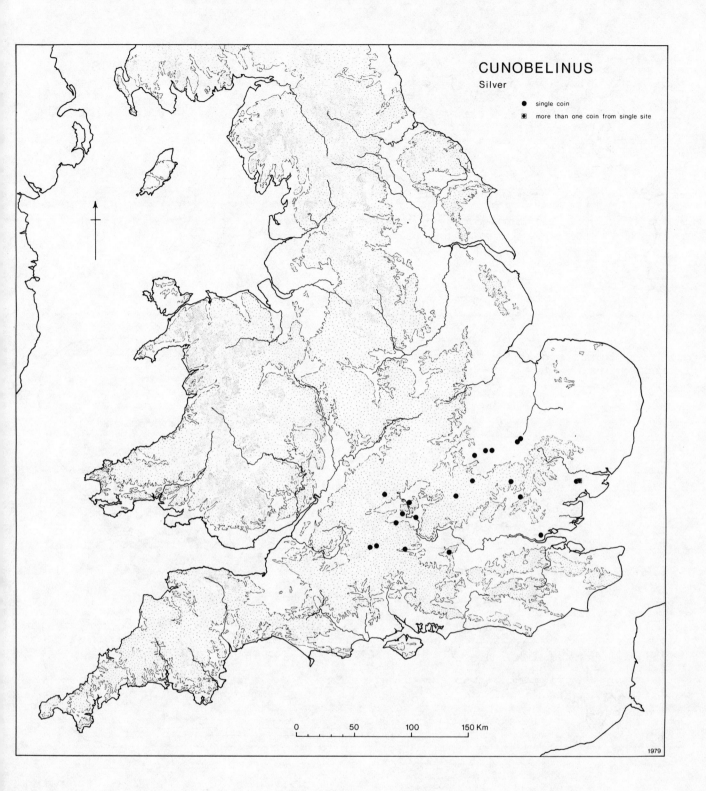

CUNOBELINUS
Silver

● single coin
▣ more than one coin from single site

0   50   100   150 Km

1979

Fig 60

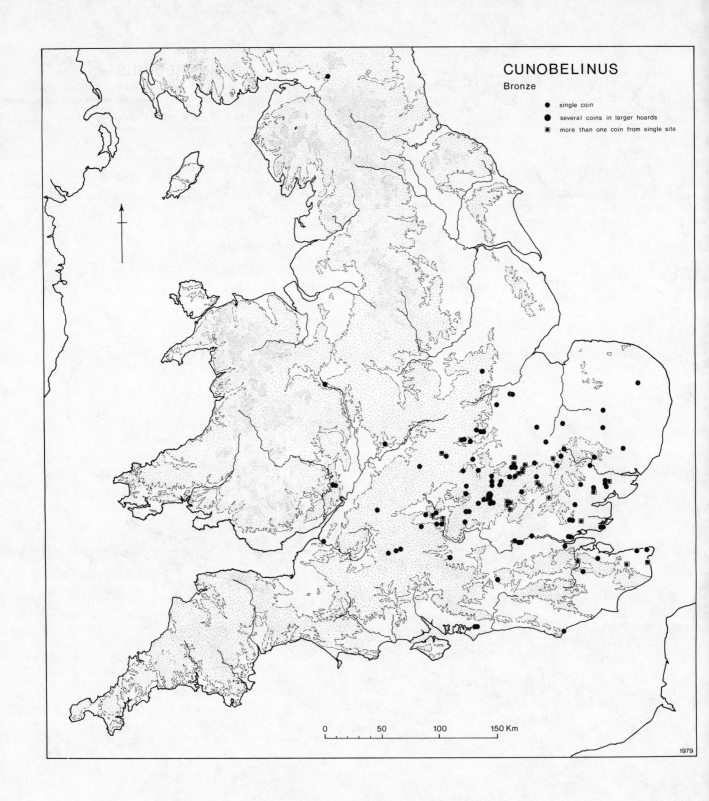

CUNOBELINUS
Bronze

● single coin
● several coins in larger hoards
▣ more than one coin from single site

0   50   100   150 Km

1979

Fig 61

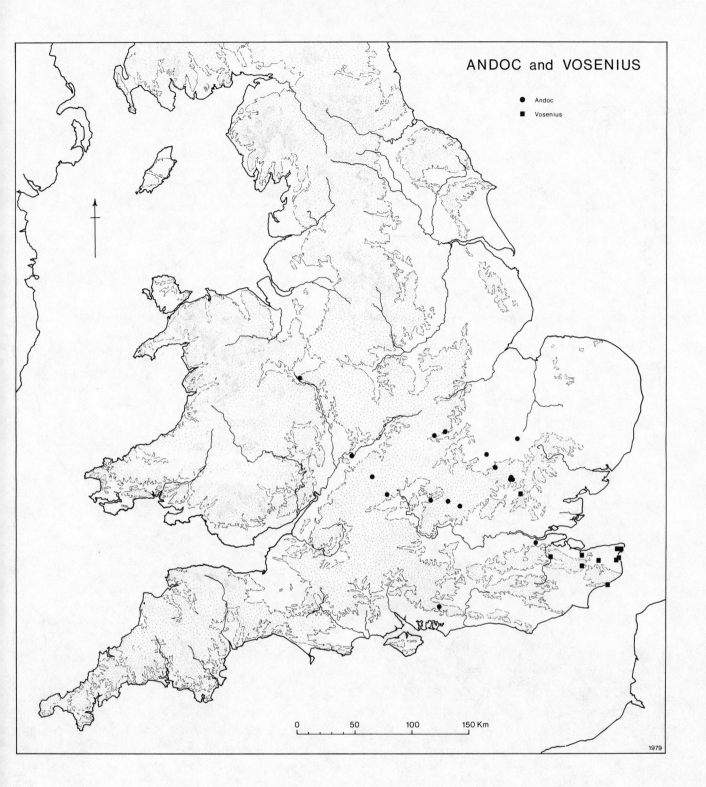

ANDOC and VOSENIUS

● Andoc
■ Vosenius

0   50   100   150 Km

1979

Fig 62

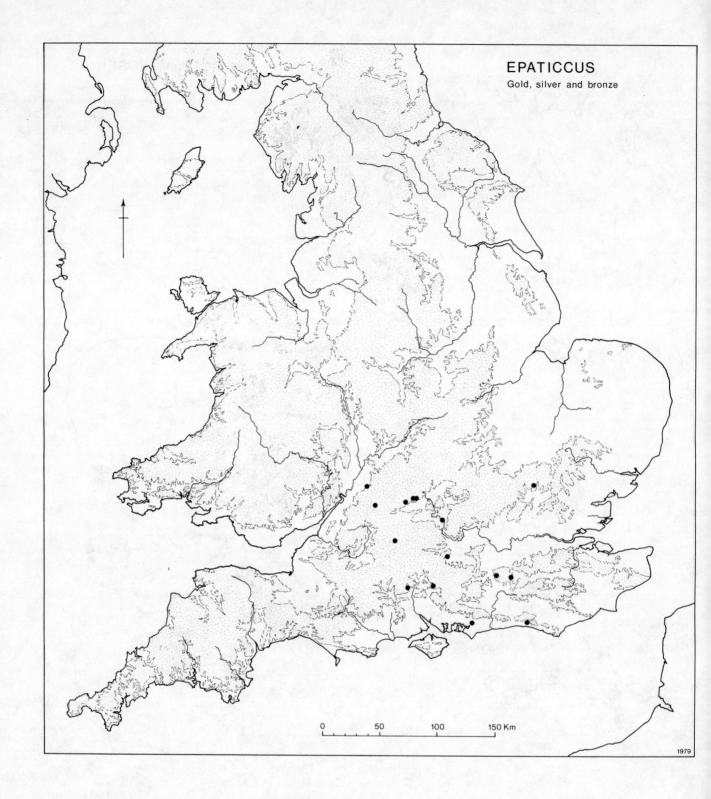

EPATICCUS
Gold, silver and bronze

0   50   100   150 Km

1979

Fig 63

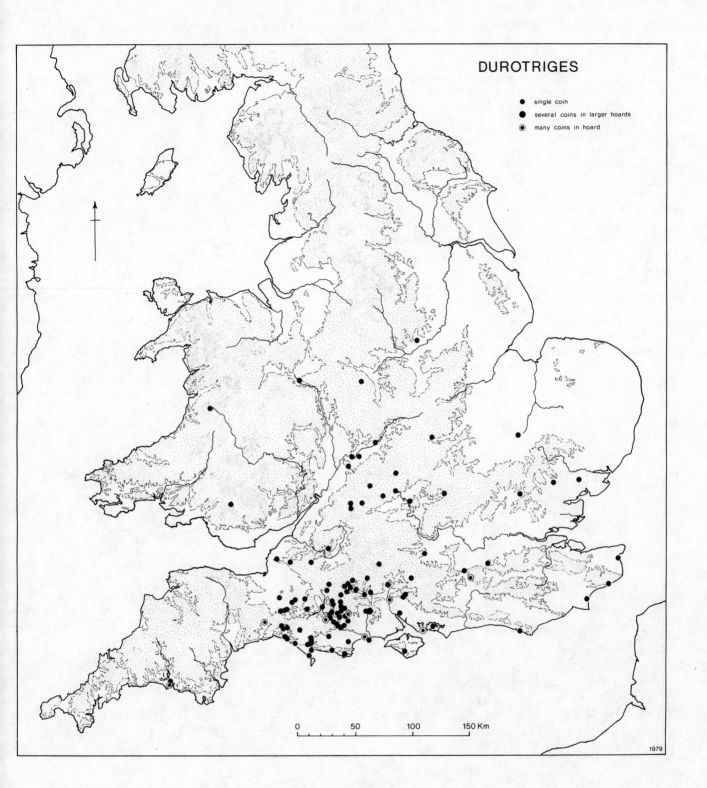

● single coin

● several coins in larger hoards

◉ many coins in hoard

0   50   100   150 Km

1979

Fig 64

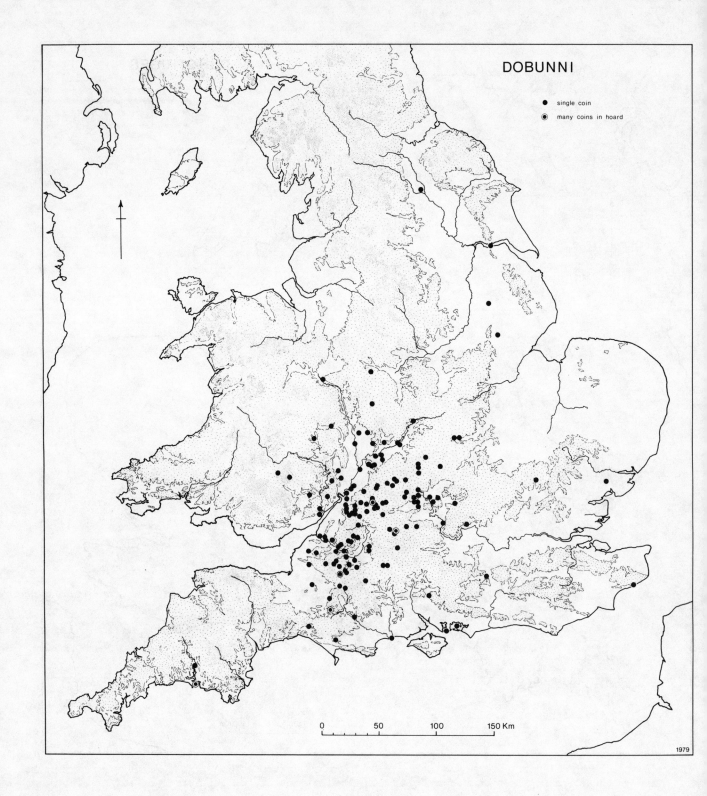

DOBUNNI

● single coin
◉ many coins in hoard

0   50   100   150 Km

1979

Fig 65

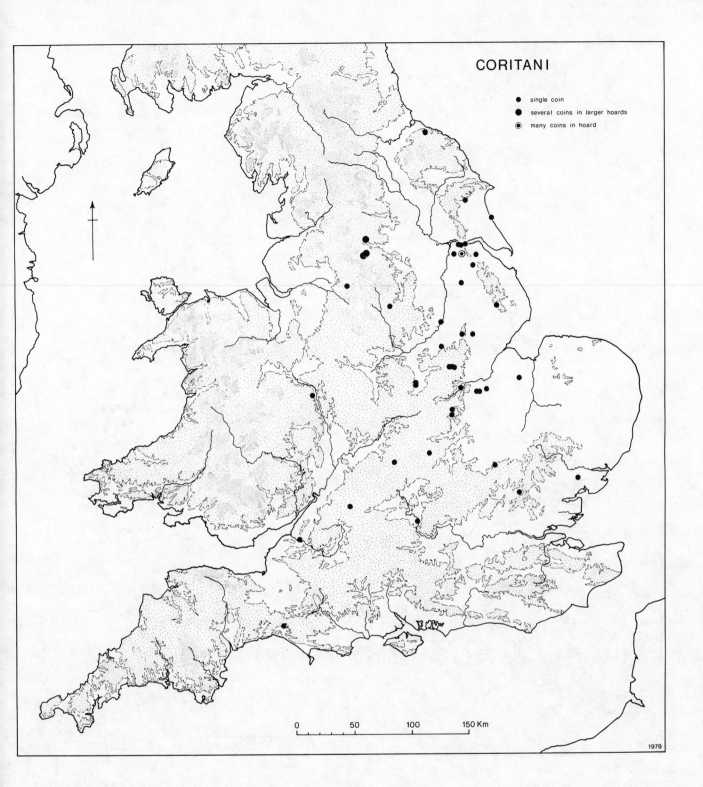

CORITANI

● single coin
● several coins in larger hoards
◉ many coins in hoard

0   50   100   150 Km

1979

Fig 66

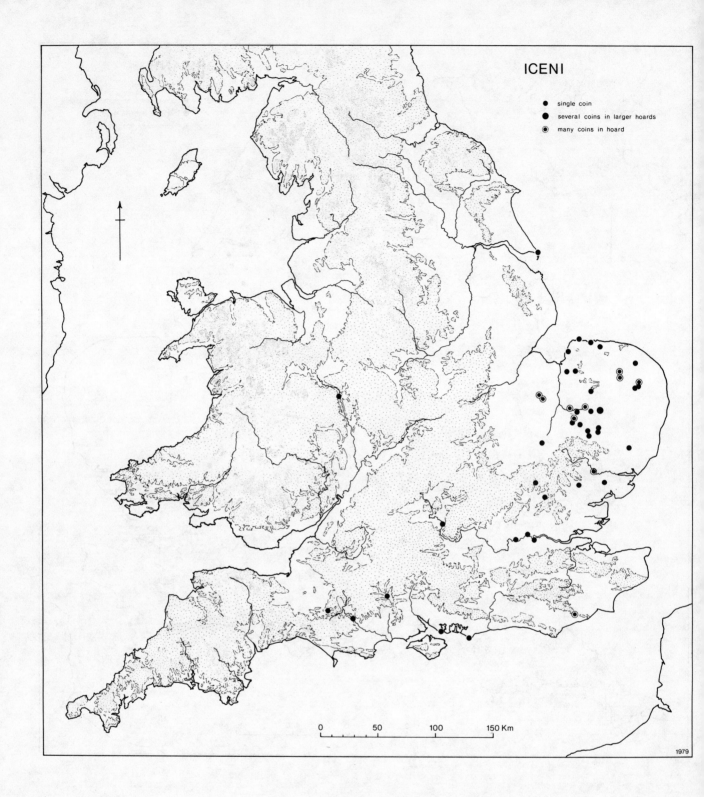

ICENI

● single coin
● several coins in larger hoards
◉ many coins in hoard

0   50   100   150 Km

1979

Fig 67

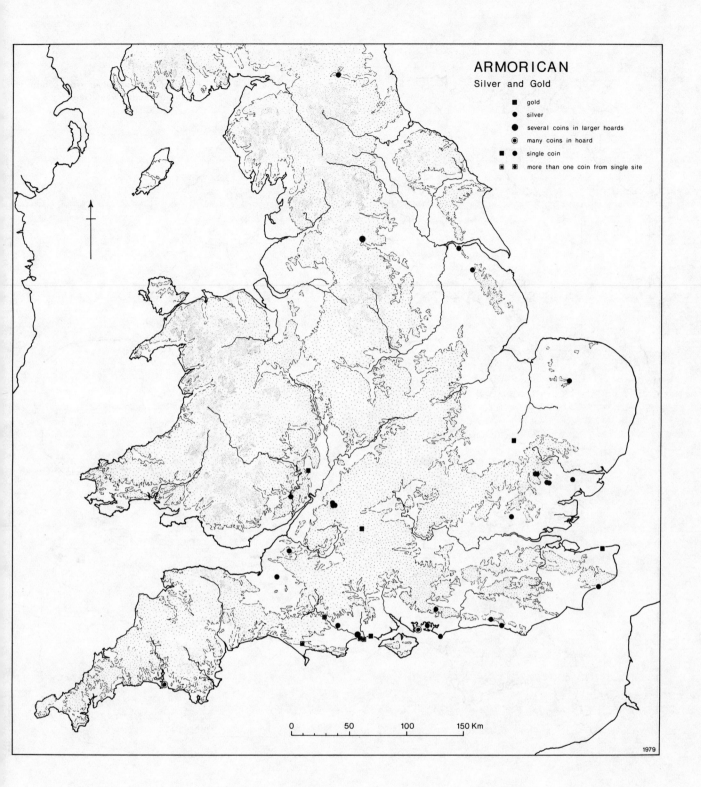

ARMORICAN
Silver and Gold

- ■ gold
- ● silver
- ⬤ several coins in larger hoards
- ◉ many coins in hoard
- ■ ● single coin
- ▣ ◉ more than one coin from single site

0   50   100   150 Km

1979

Fig 68

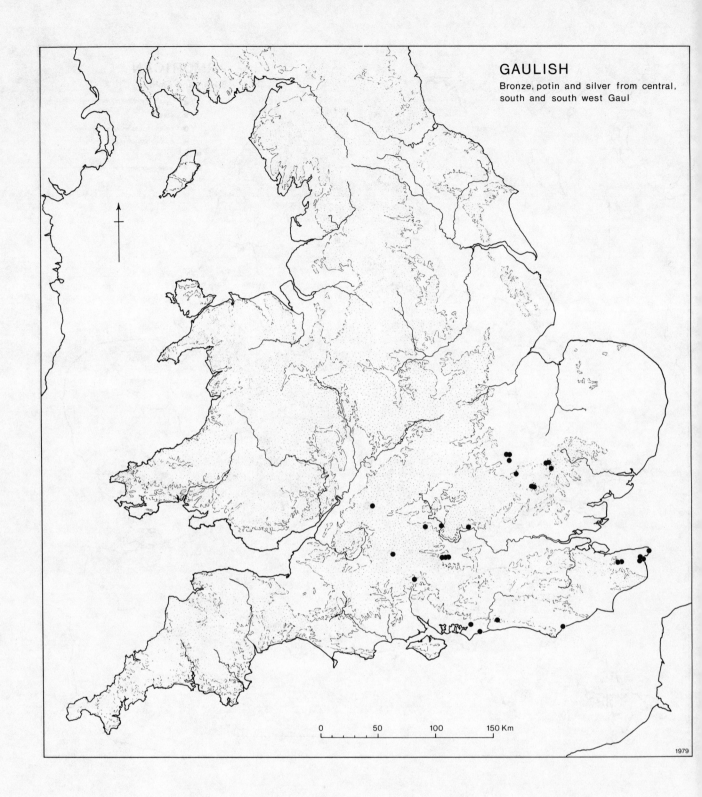

GAULISH
Bronze, potin and silver from central,
south and south west Gaul

0   50   100   150 Km

1979

Fig 69